STEVEN

Gregory B. Dickerson

authorHOUSE®

AuthorHouse™
1663 Liberty Drive
Bloomington, IN 47403
www.authorhouse.com
Phone: 1-800-839-8640

Published by AuthorHouse 2/15/2012

ISBN: 978-1-4389-7328-9 (sc)
ISBN: 978-1-4520-5885-6 (e)

This book is printed on acid-free paper.

For My Parents,

Frank and Violet Dickerson

Added photography and graphics by

John Bryant

516-413-5230
347-453-3672

WHAT THEY ARE SAYING, ABOUT 'STEVEN'

N. Davis

The Battle rages on! The Educated vs The Uneducated... Black vs Black.... A hard lesson is learned as an all too familiar theme of today's society plays out in "STEVEN", a short story by Gregory B. Dickerson on the use and meaning of the "N" word. An interesting read!

H. Williams

Great work on your book, Greg. I could not have said it better. Don't be afraid to say what is right, even though it is not popular. Your book is the gospel. I sincerely hope those in denial will stop dreaming and wake up.

A. Velasquez

My goodness, if you are interested in reading something good, I mean good, read this guy's book. His name is Gregory B. Dickerson.

M. Burns

Okay people, just read "Steven" by Gregory Dickerson. A must read!

This short story about Steven is truly an eye opener. I hate to admit, I am guilty as charged. I often use that word in what I feigned to be an affectionate term of endearment for my loved ones, even though I am fully aware of the negative inference associated with this word and in spite of the many struggles and sacrifices of those before me. Yet, I continue. People, it's time I renounce the use of that word. If there are others out there like me, stuck in a land of make believe, I incite you to obtain a copy of "Steven". I guarantee it will change your mind.

P.S. – Greg you did the damn thing. Well-written, thought-provoking, truly an eye opener. I, too, am looking forward to your next book.

Steven hates the 'N' word

As Steven

Stood on a Brooklyn, New York corner he heard

that dreadful word repeatedly

escape the mouths of two Black men

vehemently they spoke it

endorsing its coolness

numbing its listener

By Lynn V. McDonald

Inspired by

'Steven'...

The Short Story

FOREWORD

How many times have you been in a crowd of people on a street corner, at a basketball game, or maybe just in your local store and had your ears penetrated by someone using the 'N' word? One day, not so long ago, I was on a street corner standing next to two young Black men who were in deep conversation. Standing next to them for no more than two minutes, I must have heard them use the 'N' word at least twenty times in every manner you could think of. Obviously to them and others that feel the way they do, the 'N' word is an acceptable word to be used in our society. Their conversation inspired me to write my story "*Steven*." The story is about a young Black man who learns what the 'N' word means to Black people who had to endure true racism from the American society from years past. Somewhere along the way from the Civil Rights Movement with Dr. Martin Luther King, Jr., by any means necessary with Malcolm X, to President Barack Obama, we as Black people have let the most hateful word in American society become acceptable in our Black communities. I truly hope the story proves to you and others that we as African/Caribbean Americans (Black people) who had to deal with this hateful word and all it represents, should not have to endure its use for one more second in our lives and the lives of Blacks who come after us. Let us as a people bury the 'N' word once and for all.

CHAPTER ONE

On the evening of Friday, January 7, 2005, Steven Green, known as Lil Steven to his family, laid in his hand-me-down, queen-sized bed that once belonged to his parents. On this cold, windy night, relaxation did not come easily for him. Looking up at his inspiration, posters of Biggie, Tupac, and Jay-Z, admiring them was not what had his mind spinning out of control. Something more important was, his iPod, which contained their music and his irreplaceable beats that he had worked on for the past year.

It was 08:30 p.m., and the last time he had it was at 06:30 p.m., right before he had dinner. The last time he saw it was at 07:30 p.m., right there on the dresser where he had left it before he took a shower to get ready for his night out with Kim, his girlfriend.

Deciding to look around his room again for what felt like the umpteenth time, he got off the bed and onto the floor he went. Luckily for him, his carpet was plush. Therefore, he would not hurt his hands and knees. Looking under the bed, he was disappointed once more, but there was no giving up. He had to find it. Back up on his feet, he went straight for the dresser. Starting with the top drawer, he searched feverishly and did not care if he messed up the neatly folded clothes.

When he did not find it, his disappointment was so strong he felt like crying.

However, there would be none of that. 'A man is a man and men don't cry,' is what his father always said, so he continued with the search. Next were the two closets, filled with his urban wear and all of his sneakers.

When he finally finished turning the room upside down, he concluded it was gone.

"Of course. Why didn't I think of this before? The Haters. The Haters must have it," he reasoned.

He decided quickly to confront them to get it back if it was the last thing he did. Before leaving his room, he did what his father had taught him. He walked to the window and looked out at the moonlit trees blowing in the wind, which relaxed him as it always did. Steven stood there, thinking how he would approach the Haters and the words he would say to each of them. He decided to approach each one differently because each one of them was different. This was something he understood about them, but he was not sure they understood about each other. They talked the same, acted the same, but still they were different.

On the other hand, he felt like an outsider. He was the youngest of four children and five years younger than his only sister, Winsome. After she was born, their mother had her tubes tied.

"That's it. No more kids," she announced.

However, as fate would have it, five years and nine months later, Lil Steven was welcomed to the world. Closing the blinds, he turned towards the door and took a deep breath.

"This is it," he said aloud.

Steven was calmer than any twenty-year-old should be, mainly because he lived at home, drove his own car, went to college, and did not have to work. Steven had no worries. Handsome and with an athletic build, that he worked hard to maintain, Steven was more confident than his years would indicate or should allow. Walking towards the door, he heard the all-too-familiar sound of his cell phone ringing. Changing his path from the door to the dresser where the phone was, he saw a familiar name on the caller ID.

Damn! Kim. I forgot about her, he thought.

He flipped the phone open and said casually, "Hello."

"Well hello, 'S'. It's me, Kim. You remember me, don't you? Your girlfriend! And what is it you like to say to your peeps about me? Oh yeah, Kim is a bag of chips with the dip. Is that why I am here waiting for you and you didn't even call to say you are not coming? What's up with that, 'S'?"

"Easy, baby. I'm coming. I just fell asleep. I'm on my way out the door just now. I'll be there in ten minutes."

"How are you going to get here in ten minutes when you know it takes twenty minutes with no traffic? You got some bitch over there, don't you? Don't be playing me, Steven!"

"Easy, baby. Easy. You know it's all about you! Twenty minutes. I'll be there."

"You promise?"

"Yes, baby, I promise. Twenty minutes. Okay?"

"Okay, baby. Hurry up, but be careful."

CHAPTER TWO

Steven, a.k.a. Lil Steve, a.k.a. 'S', felt more than a pinch of guilt in his heart. For he knew it would take at least an hour to deal with the Haters, but Kim, the love of his life, would have to wait.

"I feel good. I look good. I'm ready," he said aloud before taking his mandatory deep breath, then exhaling slowly. Steven walked to the door and checked his reflection in the mirror. Finding everything to his liking, he opened the door and stepped carefully onto the hardwood floor, which his mother kept thoroughly cleaned and waxed.

"It was slippery as hell," he often said. With his socks on, it was like skating on ice, and he was convinced one day he would break his neck on it. He walked carefully down the hall in search of his sister, Winsome. He felt it was best to start with her, the weakest link. If he were correct, she would be in her old bedroom, admiring herself in the mirror, wishing she still lived at home instead of with her good-for-nothing husband and their two bratty kids.

He prayed she was there alone. The key to his plan was to catch each of them alone and make them feel trapped in their own web of lies, then pressure them until they realized the only way out was to tell the truth and return the iPod.

Together the Haters were like a pack of hungry wolves, and tonight, like any other Friday night, was no different: their night to get together for fish, playing cards, loud conversation, and that music. He could deal with the fish, which was not his favorite dish. He could even deal with the loud conversation. The Haters actually made him laugh.

But the music of Billie Holiday, Nat King Cole, and Fats Domino was what he could not deal with. "Who are these people my mother and father cannot get enough of?" he would ask himself. He knew this was how it always started, with the oldest of the old, and then his oldest brother, Stan, would show up with his wife and kids. Like clockwork, they were on time all the time. Before long, James Brown would be stating, "This is a man's world," and so the night would go. Then, before long, the other two would be walking through the door with their kids. Within the hour, you would think you were at Studio 54 with Donna Summer blasting from the CD player. His brother Russell was the disco freak.

Luckily for him, they couldn't hang out like they used to do. Therefore, by 11:30 p.m., he would start to hear the smooth sounds of Coltrane, Miles, Monk, Porter, and even Gato, the cool cat.

Thank God for Grandpops. He really likes all that jazz, Steven would think.

Outside of his sister's former bedroom, he could hear the voice of Keith Sweat begging on the inside. Winsome, the R&B queen was most likely pretending to be dancing up close and personal with Denzel. As long as she was in there alone, he did not care what she was doing.

Lil Steven knocked on his sister's door.

Winsome was looking at her reflection in the mirror, standing on her tiptoes as if she were wearing her three-inch pumps. She decided her ass looked fine in her fitted jeans, but she could use more time on the treadmill to help with the little bulge in the stomach.

Damn kids. Thank goodness the tits don't sag. Can't wait 'til summer to show them off again. Them brothers be tripping, she thought. Finished with the mirror, she walked across the room to the La-Z-Boy in the corner, sat down and pushed back until the footrest came out then picked up her glass of red wine off the end table.

Now why can't my life be like this every day? No annoying husband or needy kids. Hell, I would even get a job if that's what it takes.

Damn, who could that be? Pushing the chair back to its upright position and putting the glass down next to her pack of Newports, she walked to the door, asking, "Who is it?" When she reached the door, the person on the other side still had not identified him or herself.

"Who is it?" she asked again, this time more demanding.

"It's me, Steven."

"Is that you, 'S'?"

Winsome actually liked her younger brother. Although he lived a carefree life, he was very respectful of others. At twenty, he was living his life to the fullest, something she always liked about him.

The only thing she had a problem with was his choice of music. Bitches and hoes seemed to be the only words the rappers used to describe Black women. When they did say something they thought was nice, it was usually how good they gave head or how good they were in bed. One would think the Black female rapper would try to change their way of thinking, but they don't. It appears the more whorish they are, the more popular they are.

"Nah, you can keep it," she always told him.

When she opened the door, they greeted each other with a hug and kiss. It was the first time they had seen each other since her arrival. This was the reason he gave for coming to see her. After their embrace, Steven walked to the other La-Z-Boy and sat down, followed by his sister. When Winsome moved out, their parents turned the room into their own little theater. Along with the two La-Z-Boys separated by the glass table on the brown carpet, a home entertainment center consisted of a thirty-two inch flat-screen TV, a Bose CD player, and their personal computer. The room also had two sliding doors leading to a small balcony where their parents liked to sit and watch the stars on clear summer nights.

After the two reclined in the brown leather chairs, Winsome offered the under aged Steven a glass of wine. He was no stranger to alcohol, although wine was not what he preferred, but if drinking it would help get the iPod back, then so be it.

"Yes, I'll have a glass," he answered, ever so politely. Leaning forward, Winsome got a glass from the bottom shelf of the table, filled it for him, and then resumed her reclined position.

"So what's up? How you been?" she asked.

"Things have been okay," he answered, sitting up and looking at her in his sly sort of way, "but…"

Oh no. Here it comes, Winsome said to herself when she heard the word 'but.' *I knew there was more to this little visit than him just stopping by to say hello. Shit, what could he want now?*

"They could be better," he continued.

And for the first time, Winsome realized it was not a sly look of deception on his face, but a look of sadness. Wondering what was wrong with him, she sat upright in the chair. Being the type of person who did not like to see others hurting, she would sacrifice her own happiness to make someone else happy. This instinct in her was the main reason she was still with her husband of five years. Whenever she would catch him cheating or just not being there for her, she would threaten to leave. He in turn would give her that, "I'm wounded, hurt, and could never live without you," speech and she would come back to nurse his pain away.

Steven's plan was to let her see just how hurt and wounded he was, sure she would nurse his pain away by giving him the iPod back or telling him who had it. He did not think she had it, but she was with the Haters. Therefore, she had to know who did.

"Things are good, real good. Mom and dad are looking out for me. Kim and I are cool and I have no problems at school. However, sometimes I think Stan and Russell be hating on me," he told her after taking a sip of the wine, which caused Winsome's look to change from concern to 'boy, what are you talking about?'

"I try to confide in them, tell them how I feel about my life and the things I want to do, but they don't care about how I feel, like you do," he continued, not surprised by her look.

"Well, how do you feel? And what do you want to do with your life?"

"Mostly it's about school. I've been thinking about taking some time off to pursue my dream," he said, thinking all he had to do was tell her what she wanted to hear so she would tell him what he needed to know.

"Now, what dream are we talking about?" she demanded, standing up and looking down at him as if he were crazy, causing his heart to sink into his stomach.

"I want to stop going to school so I can concentrate on being a rapper," he said finally after coughing to clear his throat, stalling not wanting to answer the question.

"A rapper? Stop going to school?" she said before she tossed her head back then walked to the window and opened the blinds. She looked out into the night sky as if to be praying.

"Yes, a rapper," she heard him say again. "Russell and Stan both know it. That's why they took my iPod with all my music. And you know they have it, don't you?"

"What makes you think I don't have it? You know no one in this house can understand why you would involve yourself with anything glorifying the 'N' word. That also degrades women and is the root cause for so much negative thinking, along with, as we all know, violence in the Black community. To top it off, you and your friends damn near worship a White dude for it! So what makes you think I don't have it?" she asked calmly after turning away from the window with a look of conviction on her face. "I'm going to get some fish. You coming?" she continued, not giving him a chance to answer and not caring what he had to say.

'*She just may have it*', he thought, as he got up to follow her downstairs.

CHAPTER THREE

Exiting the room, once again Steven was careful of his footing on the hallway floor. Turning left, he headed for the staircase, holding tightly onto the banister before going down the stairs. He always held on because he found the stairs to be as slippery as the floors.

When he finally reached the bottom of the stairs, he heard an unusual sound for this time of night on a Friday—quiet, no music playing, no loud talking or laughter.

"Shit, what are they up to now?" he asked himself before he turned down the hallway, passing the old pictures of Dr. Martin Luther King, Jr. and John F. Kennedy. The living room was on his left and the dining room on the right. He went straight into the kitchen, where all of his family members were sitting at the table in deep conversation.

When they realized he was standing there, silence overcame the room. Steven just stood there, not knowing what to say.

'Damn, how did Winsome get down here so fast without breaking her neck and what did she say to them?'

"Well, come on, little rapper man. Tell everybody your big plans," Winsome said with slurred speech after she finished her third glass of wine and poured her fourth.

All eyes were on him. He stood dry-mouthed with nothing to say, looking at the people who had done so much for him. Together they pitched in financially to pay for his education, keep a roof over his head and put clothes on his back. Steven was well-supported and did not have to work, which allowed him to concentrate on his studies. They were people of modest means, but they decided a long time ago that he would attend college. The family came up with a plan to pool their money when he was very young, and the plan was working.

The one thing they did not plan on, however, was how he felt. Now that he was getting older, he had his own plans, and they were not what his family had in mind for him. He knew he had to tell them, but not at this time. Telling Winsome was only part of his plan to get the iPod back.

'Shit, she is blowing me up. How do I get out of this without losing their help?' was his only thought.

Sitting next to his mother, he picked up a piece of fish from the serving dish in the middle of the table. With his head down, he took a bite, and then looked up with a mouthful, asking, "What?" of his family that still had their eyes on him.

"Your sister may be full of wine, but we're all sure she didn't leave Keith what's-his-name to come down here to tell us a bunch of lies about you," his father told him after everyone either rolled their eyes or sucked their teeth at him. "Boy, what is going on in that little head of yours?" he asked, standing to his full six feet, then placing his hands on the table.

There was complete silence in the room as his father stood staring at him. He had refinanced the mortgage on the house not once, but *twice* to help pay for Steven's schooling, and he was not about to let his or the others' investment fall through the cracks. The rest of the family became increasingly more uncomfortable as the tension grew. Winsome put her glass on the table and folded her arms over her chest. She was wishing she had stayed upstairs with Keith.

Steven put his uneaten fish on a napkin, finally deciding to say something, but before he could get the words out, his oldest brother Stan spoke first.

"So," he started, "you want to be a gangsta rapper, spreading more negativity into the hood with your nigga this and nigga that? Yeah, I know how you talk when you're with your homies, with your pants hanging off your ass."

"Look, nobody is saying you have to be a nerd. But don't think we are going to let you start running the streets so we can find you dead somewhere or in jail. After all the hard work you put in, why would you want to stop? Why? We don't understand!"

'This is how it always is when they don't agree with something I want to do. Well, this time it's going to be different. They are going to listen to me,' Steven thought to himself, sitting there looking calm on the outside, but very upset on the inside.

Pushing his chair away from the table, he heard Russell's voice. *'Shit,'* crossed his mind before he could stand.

"So what you going to do, lil' bro? Get you a deal and go on the road with the rest of the wannabees? Do you know how many cats like you are trying to make it big? And here you are, damn near number one in your class, talking about trying to be down," he said, as he walked from the opposite side of the table to the back of Steven's chair.

"I've been in them streets. Look how long it took me to get my shit straight," he whispered in his ear loud enough for all to hear. "I was there when this whole rap thing started. It was dangerous then and one hundred percent more dangerous now. I guess you want to keep it real? Well then, let's keep it real. The rap game is the new drug game. You know it and we know it, and look at where those drugs got us. Stan will always walk with a limp, and this scar," he continued, pointing to his forehead, "will never go away. Is that what you want to be a part of? I've listened to your rap. Yeah, I know how to work an iPod," he continued as Winsome did, not waiting for an answer. "All it amounts to is the same old gangsta bullshit. So, you want to be another menace to society?"

'Menace to society? What the hell is he talking about?' Steven thought, while he watched his brother walk back to the opposite side of the table and his father sit back down.

The room became quiet again. All Steven could hear were the kids running up and down the stairs, in and out of the rooms, playing a game of tag no one would normally let them play. But 'The Haters' were too busy saving his life. He just sat there, wanting to say everything that was on his mind, but he knew they were not finished. His mother and maybe even grand pop would have something to say. For sure his mother, and as if she had read his mind, she stood up then walked in Winsome's direction.

"Girl, don't let this upset you. We are people who care about each other," she told her, before she freshened up her glass, and then handed it to her. "We 'check' each other. Is that the right word, 'S'? Check?" she asked, looking in his direction and like those before her, not needing or wanting an answer.

"Yes, I know you're known as 'S' outside of this house. How you act, how you wear your oversized pants and shirts. The people you be with, that we all know are up to no good. Baby, all that is okay with me even if you want to stop going to school and get a job, or just do something else with yourself. Even your music!"

Up until he heard the word music, he really was not paying much attention, but maybe she would say something he wanted to hear, he hoped.

"I know about rap," she continued. "Now me, I don't like it. Plain and simple. But when I was coming up, there was music your grandfather didn't like that he let me listen to. So, who am I to stop you from rapping if that's what you want?"

"However, understand one thing, young man. If you wish to stop going to school to become a gangster rapper, or whatever you call it, you will not be living under this roof! I know all about the money and the exciting lifestyle, but baby, there is too much negativity involved with it for this family. Tell me, have you ever heard the 'N' word used in this house? But hey, you're a big boy and I'm sure you will do what's best. Now, why don't you go put my song on. You know the one I like. It's still Friday night and I want to dance with your father!"

With that, she walked to her husband and took him by the hand and pulled him out of the chair.

Lil Steven, being the good son, walked into the living room to put the song on, when from behind he heard a voice call out to him.

"Steven, where's that iPod thing you always have on your head?"

The voice was that of his grandfather. Turning around only to see his back going up the stairs, he turned back to the CD player as his parents and brothers paired off with their mates on the living room floor. They may not have liked his music, but they kept him as the DJ for theirs. When the CD was fully loaded, he pressed the skip button until it reached track number eight. When the Dells started singing, 'Oh What a Night,' he turned for the stairs, still in search of the iPod.

Reaching the stairs, he grabbed onto the banister, taking one step at a time. His niece and nephew ran down quickly, which made him think:

Why is it everyone can get around this house as fast as they like except me?

Shaking his head, he kept heading up the stairs. Midway up, he looked over his shoulder at the Haters on their makeshift dance floor, asking himself:

How could such loving people be so hateful?

CHAPTER FOUR

At the top of the stairs, he turned right, heading straight for his grandfather's room, along the way encountering more yelling and running nephews and nieces. Normally he would play with them, but not tonight. Once at the door, he could still hear the high-pitched voices of the kids. With his hand raised, about to knock, he heard the voice of his grandfather tell him:

"The door is open, Steven. Come in."

The sound of the voice surprised him so much he just stood there with his hand raised until he noticed his nephew, John, staring up at him. Looking back at him, he opened the door and entered the room. John watched his every move until the door closed.

"Boy, you look like you just saw a ghost. What's wrong with you?"

"I'm okay," he responded, walking to the empty seat in the corner of the room. After a second, he was able to relax, noticing his surroundings and the smell of the cigar his grandfather was smoking as he laid on the bed. He was propped up on the pillows, his legs crossed, sipping Johnny Walker Black, with Coltrane playing softly in the background. At eighty years old, yet looking like sixty, he was still drinking, smoking, and hearing through doors.

Damn, he still the man, Steven almost said out loud, looking at him through the blue haze of the smoke.

"What you going to do, Steven?" his grandfather asked.

"I am going to go on the road, Pops. With my crew. This is our time. We can make it big. I know we can this summer. That is why I can't go back to school this semester. We need to practice full time, do the small clubs so we can get ready. Look, I know you don't know about this type of music, but the streets are feeling us. We got an agent who is down with the groups that'll be on the big tours this summer. He thinks we can get down as an opening act if we're ready. I'm telling you we can blow up!"

Now Steven was actually 'S', moving his hands in street fashion, each word louder than the one before. Pops was really enjoying the show, lying back, not having moved an inch.

"And to answer your question, no I don't know where my iPod is. It has been missing for hours and I don't think it is lost," he said sitting back down, saying these words with anger in his voice.

"If you don't think it's lost, what do you think happened to it?"

"The truth?"

"It will set you free."

"Well, before everyone said what they had to say about rap, I wasn't sure if one of them had it, but now I'm convinced of it." Standing up again, he paced back and forth, gesturing with his hands. "Everyone is in on it. I don't know what their problem is anyway. Man, they're the ones always telling me to express myself, about free speech and all that other shit they be talking. Now look what happens. Everybody gets on my case about what I have to say, then steal my music, and you know that shit ain't right!"

"Come sit over here and pour me a drink," Pops told him after he stopped talking and before he could sit.

Steven looked at him for some type of response, hoping Pops would agree with him. Picking up the bottle off the end table, which was actually closer to Pops, he poured him a drink, and then sat down. He sat in the chair trying to relax waiting for Pops to speak, praying he would agree with him and help get the iPod back. But mostly he wanted him to take his side, so he could help get the Haters to change their minds about his plans. Steven was no fool about his life. Until now, the Haters were paying his way and he did not want that to stop. He had not told them his whole plan. Not only did he want to stop going to school, but he also did not plan on getting a job or moving out of the house. He figured, since they were investing in his education, the investment could be changed to his skills. Steven was sure the payoff would be greater and come a lot faster. However, the idea did not look too good with the way they were thinking. There was no way he could get them to change their minds, but maybe, just maybe, Pops, with his influence, could. Steven just sat there, waiting for him to speak, praying his speech had worked.

After finishing his drink, Pops placed the glass back on the table, slid his legs over the edge of the bed, and turned his upper body to face Steven.

"Do you know who this is playing?" he asked, putting his cigar butt in the ashtray, then placing his hand under Steven's chin to raise his head until their eyes met.

"John. John Coltrane. Your favorite jazz artist. You listen to him all the time."

"That's right. He's my main man. He could do anything with his horn. Too bad he died at such a young age. What a shame."

"How old was he when he died?"

"Forty or forty-one, I think. I'm really not sure. I do know them drugs got him. Yeah, he had it bad. There were a lot of artists hooked on that stuff back then, and you're right, I don't know about rap. So why don't you tell me what the artists of today are hooked on?"

"What do you mean?" he asked nervously, knowing deep down inside what he meant.

"What do I mean?" he responded, letting his face go, and pouring himself another drink. "Steven, I may be old, still drink and smoke, but I still have my senses. Shit, I knew downstairs you would come to me, and I know what you want me to do."

"What would I look like if I told them to let you drop out of school so you can go on the road with your crew? To do what? Smoke weed, maybe do some coke, and for damn sure drink too much alcohol? Yeah, I know what rappers are hooked on. Boy, don't you understand when I was your age how hard it was for people like me to get an education? And in case you don't know it, I never did. Had to teach myself what little I do know. That's why I made sure your mother went to school and she feels the way she does about you going."

"Now, about this rap?" he asked, as he walked to the CD player to turn the music off.

"Pops, it's like this. Just like Mom said. When she was coming up there was music the older people didn't like that the younger people did. But nowadays, these older people think they can tell us everything about life, especially our music," he answered, not believing his ears, always thinking Pops was different. Now here he was saying the same shit as them, he thought to himself.

"So, what is the problem with your music?"

"There is no problem. That's the point. They just be bugging because of some of the words. Most of them are the same words they use every day, but they have a problem when we use them in our music. What's up with that?"

"If you tell me some of the words, maybe I could tell you what's up with that."

Now how do I tell this eighty-year-old man, my grandfather, the answer to his question is fuck, bitch, hoe, pussy, dick, and the most used, nigga. Now how do I tell him that?

He knew Pops wanted an answer, and if there were any chance of getting his help, he would have to give him one.

"Would they be fucking, bitch, and the main one, nigger? Words such as these?"

"Yes," he answered, with his head down.

"Then you know nobody in this house is going to deal with it, and you know how I feel. Boy, I'm eighty years old. Do you know Blacks in my day died to get people to stop using that word, and here you come complaining to me that we don't want you to use it!"

They looked at each other, their minds on the same thing, yet their thoughts were worlds apart. Pops walked slowly to him, gently taking his face in his hands, and let the word flow ever so gently off his tongue, "Nigger."

Letting his face go, he walked to the window. "That word and that word alone made most of my life pure hell. What you fail to understand is what it really means, meant, and will always represent to those who don't see us for the people we are, but only for the color of our skin! Do you know what it is like not to be allowed to drink water on the hottest day of the year because the colored-only fountain is not working? Always having to sit in the back of the bus, always having to go through the back door of every public building your tax money helped build! Did you know I was pretty good at baseball?" he asked after taking a deep breath trying to compose himself and not wanting Steven to see him getting upset.

"No, I didn't. No one ever told me you played any sport."

"Well, I did. No one told you because pretty good is not good enough to be remembered in any day an' age. But even if I were the Michael Jordan of baseball back then, the powers that be would not have let my black ass play in their league. Why? Because my ass is black! Young man, you could never in your wildest dreams understand the hate those people had!" Pops yelled, unable to maintain his cool.

"That was then. This is now. Why can't people like you let go of the past?" Steven yelled back, not showing any remorse or feeling of concern. He did not care how Pops felt or why he felt the way he did. Just like most young Blacks, he did not care about the injustice Blacks before him endured. With sarcasm in his voice, he let his words come out of his mouth slowly and deliberately to be sure he heard and understood every one of them.

"Blacks, Whites, all people now go to the same schools, hospitals, clubs, and stores, and even share the same water fountains!" Rising out of the seat, he moved slowly to Pops, still speaking in the same manner.

Pops stood his ground, not knowing what he might do. He prayed Steven did not hit him.

"Why can't you and the rest of them understand the word nigga is not the same for us? Everybody says it, but I don't see anyone being killed because of it!"

"Nigga, nigga, nigga, and more nigga," he said repeatedly in Pops' face, close enough to smell the liquor on his breath.

Pops continued to hold his ground, not letting on he was frightened to death.

Finally, Steven turned away, still saying the word he seemed to love the most. Opening the door, he snarled one more time, "Nigga," then walked out of the room, leaving the door open behind him.

CHAPTER FIVE

Stomping down the hallway, Steven headed for his room when his six-year-old nephew, David, ran up to him and slapped him on the arm then yelled, "Tag, you're it," in a high-pitched voice sending chills through Steven's body. Coming out of his anger-induced trance to see five of his nephews and nieces running and yelling in different directions, he paused for a second. He then decided to stay angry and finished stomping to his room. At the door, he turned to look at the kids who in turn looked at him, until he opened the door and then slammed it closed.

At the sound of the door slamming, the kids, as if on cue, started yelling and chasing each other around again.

Inside, he stood with his back against the door, his head raised with his hands covering his eyes, unable to believe what he had just did. Pops was truly his friend, the only one in the family he could talk with when he needed someone to listen to him.

"Now what?" he said aloud. His anger subsiding, Steven decided he would go back and apologize to Pops, not for what was said or how he felt, but for the way he said it. Lowering his head, he removed his hands from his eyes and noticed the mess he had made in search of the iPod.

He may have been your average twenty-year-old, but his mother, Ruby, was not your average mother when it came to the cleanliness of her house. Cleaning was one of the first things he remembered learning to do. Her mother taught her at a very early age that poor people, such as themselves, had to take care of what little they had. This way of life she passed onto him and his siblings.

Although his first eight years were spent in one of the most crime-filled housing projects the city had to offer, his family's Saturday mornings were spent like no other families he knew of, no matter what time of year it was. He could still remember being awakened from a sound sleep by the cool and sometimes cold air. She would open every window in the apartment. 'Airing out the house,' she would call it. Her favorite music would be playing as loud as the old stereo could stand it, and if you were not out of your bed in ten minutes after the cold air chilled your room, she would come in and pull the covers and sheets off of you.

When you were up, you had two choices. The first was to help clean the house, which included washing the walls, mopping the floors, washing the clothes at the laundromat (which could take hours), or the second, cleaning anything else she deemed dirty. Alternatively, you could leave, which no one chose to do because no one had a place to go. And if you did, you would have to come home and deal with her bodyguard—Winston Green, her husband, his dad.

At six feet tall, 200 pounds with a muscular build, he was very capable for the job. And with his undying love for her, they didn't stand a chance when it came to defying her. If he thought one of them was not doing as she said, he would just give them 'that look' and that would be the end of it. To this day, he never put his hands on any of them in anger, because they never gave him a reason.

If they had been a team, she would have been the owner, and he the coach, with the kids as players who never got off the bench until told to do so. With her five-foot-five inch frame, one would never think she could control this man the way she did or the way he let her think she did. If she made an unwise decision, instead of fighting over it, he would just correct the problem in the end. This, he said, kept the peace in the house and the love in their marriage. Although they both worked, they never made a lot of money. And with four mouths to feed, what they did make did not go very far. So when she told him she did not want to live in the projects any longer and wished for them to own their own home, he felt their relationship had come to a crossroads, one at which he was determined not to take the wrong turn.

Ruby would not leave him if he could not get them a house—he was sure—but unhappiness was something he felt she should never have to feel. His love for her ran so deep he would do everything in his power to make her happy. Her unhappiness was something he could not accept.

It took about a year, but they did it. First, he took on a second job, along with anyone over the age of eighteen still living in the house having to start paying rent. This meant Stan, the oldest at nineteen, started paying, all of which was put into a bank account he opened in his and her name, along with all the money he made from the second job. After talking with the banker, they found this was enough for a ten percent down payment on a house valued at one hundred thousand dollars. The price was well within what he had in mind, but well below her expectations. She, being the bigger dreamer, had her mind set on the American dream, a white-picket-fenced house in the suburbs. He, being the more realistic of the two, figured the fixer-upper down the block would be just fine. The family would still be in the area they lived in all of their lives, and there would be no financial change for them, traveling back and forth to work.

When he took her to see the house, she could not believe her eyes. Figuring he had finally lost his mind, she told him so. He knew he was taking a chance with this, but he had a plan. The house was an old brownstone on the corner of the block. Therefore, it had more square footage than the others. However, it was old and in need of more than just a coat of paint.

This was his problem. How could he get Ruby to go along with his plan without her becoming terribly unhappy? Promising himself he would never do that to her, but given the opportunity, he could make her happy beyond her wildest dreams. This house may not have been in the suburbs, but to him it was a gold mine. Ruby could not see this and he could not blame her. How could she see passed the boarded-up top two floors with its three bedrooms, two bathrooms, living room, dining room, a kitchen actually big enough to walk around in, and all those windows? No, she could not see it, but he was sure she did see the middle floor, which was also boarded up, with its two-bedroom apartment, or the first-floor one-bedroom apartment someone was paying to rent.

No, he was sure she did not see it.

Maybe, he hoped, she did see the small balcony off the room in the back, with all of those trees in the big back yard. Maybe, just maybe, she saw what he saw: potential. If only he could get her inside to see the hardwood floors, that might do it. However, she had to know the brick she was looking at would last another hundred years. She had to know that. He saw it for what it was: an investment opportunity they could not pass up, one he had to make her see.

They walked slowly back to their apartment, not saying a word or holding hands as they usually did, each thinking of a way to get the other to see things his or her way. When they walked into the apartment, the kids, who had been waiting for them to come home with the good news of where they would be moving to, could tell by the looks on their faces something was wrong.

Ruby came through the door first, only to see four smiling faces turn to frowns. Bowing her head while tightly wrapping her arms around herself, she turned left and quickly walked passed the small kitchen on her right. She headed for one of the three bedrooms as the tears started to roll gently down her face.

The kids, who had rarely seen their mother cry, sat with their mouths open as their father came through the door. He followed her, but stopped when he felt the cold stares of his children on his back. Looking back at them, he was sure their icy stares would be gone, but the three pairs of eyes were still looking at him in contempt.

His three oldest children were sure he was the reason for their mother's unhappiness. Steven, his youngest son, hid behind Winsome, holding her leg. He did not know what was going on. Winston released a deep breath and shook his head at them. He turned to walk down the hallway, with a heavy heart, in search of his wife. Walking down the dimly lit hallway, he heard Steven calling out to him from behind.

"What's wrong with Mommy, Daddy?" he asked when his father bent down to pick him up.

"She is just a little sad right now, but I will make her happy again," he answered, putting him back down. "Now go back in the living room with your brothers and sister."

"You promise?" he asked before doing as he was told.

"Yes, I promise!" They looked into each other's eyes for a very long moment before Steven finally turned and ran back into the living room.

Knocking gently on the bedroom door that he and his wife shared, Winston waited a second or two for an answer. When one was not forthcoming, he entered the room to find her lying on the bed, still crying.

"Baby, why you so upset?" he asked, sitting beside her on the bed, rubbing her back.

"How could you?" she wanted to know, sitting up with her back against the headboard, turning to face him.

"How could I what?"

"After all we've been through. After all the pain."

He got up off the bed as she spoke, starting to understand why she was so upset. At the only window in the room, he stood looking out at the kids playing on the playground as she continued to speak. The room was small with only the bed, two dressers for furnishings, and one closet they both shared for what little clothes they had.

"Do I really have to tell you? Or have you forgotten what has been going on with this family? Or do you prefer not to care?"

"Yes, I do care. You know I do."

"So why don't you do something about it? Do you really believe they are paying Stan that kind of money to sell cigarettes and milk in that bodega? I can't stand the place," she said with as much nastiness as she could muster. "What about school? Do you think he is going to even try to get his GED with the money they pay him? Is he going to work for those Colombians until someone comes in that damn drug den and blows his brains out? Yes, we took the money, but does it mean we have to keep ignoring where it really comes from? Yes, I know what goes on down there. So don't even look at me like that!"

"What about Russell? Seventeen years old with only enough credits to be considered a freshman, and if he comes in here high one more time, his ass is out," she continued, getting off the bed to stand next to him. "I'm tired of it, Winston. Dead tired. Oh yeah, you're going to be a grandfather. That's right. His little girlfriend hasn't seen her period in two months. And guess who wants birth control pills?" Winston had turned to look at her, but returned to the window, watching the neighborhood thugs who showed up to their usual spot at their usual time. The two groups of thugs were now having a heated discussion outside the window.

"Right again," she answered for him, "your little girl, Winsome."

When she was like this, he knew to just let her go on until she was finished, no matter how bad it was. He continued to look at the thugs, whose disagreement had become a full-scale shouting match.

"Winston, have you taken a good look at her lately, trying to walk around here half-naked with her chest hanging out? I spend more time running behind her, trying to make sure she got decent clothes on more than anything else. Boys, boys, boys! That's all she thinks about, Winston," she said more softly, taking him by the hand. "Baby, them two boys think they are men now. Soon they will be, but Steven and Winsome, they're still young. We still have a chance to get them out of here, away from all this violence, drugs, and gangs. We owe them the chance to get a good education and a decent life."

Turning away from the brewing brawl outside his first floor apartment window—a scene he was all too familiar with—made him wonder if the only thing they had to do was fight over who would sell drugs in front of his window.

"Woman, don't you ever accuse me of not providing a good life for you and those kids," he said, snatching his hand from hers while stepping away from the window. "What you think if we move out to the suburbs with the White folk, they gonna be better off?"

"Yes," she answered in a voice loud enough to be heard outside the room.

"Well, you can move out there if you want to, but me and my kids are staying right here with our people. Yeah, I know how bad it is here, but this is all I know. Believe me. It's not going to stay this way. I'm telling you this drug thing is not going to be like this forever, and when it's gone, the good will come back. That's why we need to stay here and invest in our community, not theirs. In ten years, that house we can get now for a hundred thousand will be worth a hell of a lot more, just trust me."

"Ten years? Are you crazy? All of us will be dead, but not me and my kids. Winston, we're not dying here at the hands of them crackheads and drug dealers, but you can if you want to!"

"Oh, damn it, woman," he said just as loud, "nobody is going to kill us."

It was not loud enough, however, to drown out the shattering of the window as the bullets came through.

CHAPTER-SIX

Sitting on his window bench with the back of his head against the cold window, Steven couldn't help but to think the thoughts he always thought when he was this mad at the Haters. Thoughts so disturbing, they often haunted him for days afterwards. However, this time he was sure they would not. The disturbing thoughts, he decided, needed to be played out if he ever was to become what he wanted to be. It was clear to him after the night's events the Haters' hate for him ran too deep. They would never let go of their grip on him, to let him be what he knew he was to become.

They were holding him back, he often thought, and for that they had to be removed. Removed in such a way he could still benefit from what they had to offer financially, part of which he felt he was entitled to anyway. This would not be necessary, he would often think if some of the events in the past had played out just a little differently. An inch here, a foot there, and they would not be here.

Why did he step back from the window? That's what I always wanted to know. How could three .44-caliber bullets have missed him? Luck, it had to be the same dumb luck that saved Stan's dumb ass. The reason he still walks with a limp, I should have told Russell, is because the doctors couldn't remove all the bullets from his back. One inch to the left and his spine would have been blown out. He should have known those stick-up kids were coming into that store. Shit, they got everybody else before him. What made him think he was different? Greed. That's all it was. Those Colombians were paying him well to sell their shit and he didn't care if he lived or died doing it, so why should I?

Most unbelievable to him was not how the two cheated death that year, but how all three of them did. Russell, not long after the bullets came through the window and into Stan's back, decided he would be mister tough guy. He went looking for and found the shooters who took the window out. The only problem was they were a lot tougher than he.

God only knows why they did not kill him. Two weeks later, when he finally awoke from the coma they put him in, he found a scar which will grace his head for the rest of his life. What really pissed Steven off these last five years was when he found out, before the bullets came through the window, his parents were having an argument their marriage would not have recovered from. Had they split, their mother alone, most likely, would have raised them. With the way things were, there would have been no way she could have controlled them the way their father did. He would have been, he felt, free to do what he wanted to do.

At fifteen, Winsome, figured it was time he knew why their family was over protective, told him every detail of their family's history over the last ten years.

She began with the day their parents came through the door with looks of despair on their faces, to the very day she was telling it. The drug use, the drug money, the lack of education and the infidelities of their father, something no one ever spoke about. She went to great lengths to be sure he understood just what happened the day the bullets came. She explained to him their mother was determined to move out of the projects to get him and her away from the drugs and violence. Their father was equally determined to stay close to them to benefit from the real estate boom he believed was to come.

She told him how she could hear the window being shattered by the bullets causing all of the kids to run into the room finding their parents taking cover in each other's arms on the floor. Their mother vowed immediately to stay with their father, no matter what he did or wherever he wanted to live, just as long as he promised her he would protect Steven and Winsome.

"I'll be whatever I want to be and talk any way I want to talk. Fuck them niggas. I'll be a god damn menace to society if I want to be," Steven said, looking at himself in the mirror more determined than ever to get out of their grip. "Nigga this, nigga that, nigga, nigga what!" he yelled at the top of his lungs while walking slowly towards the door. He turned and laid back against it, raised his head, and with his eyes closed, let out a deep breath.

Then, he opened his eyes slowly.

When they focused, he could not believe what he was seeing on top of the dresser.

The iPod. Right where he left it!

Not knowing what to think and becoming nervous, he walked slowly on shaky legs to the dresser and picked it up as if he had never seen one before. Holding it gently in his hands, he looked for the chipped corner that would tell him if it was indeed his, a chip caused from dropping it one too many times.

"Yes, yes, yes," he repeated once the corner was found.

"Damn, where you been all night?" he asked it as if it could speak. Feeling his heart racing with excitement, he decided to lay on the bed to listen to one song to help relax his nerves before going to pick up Kim. Walking to the bed, he placed the earphones in his ears, pressed the play button, climbed on the bed, rolled onto his back, and then stretched out waiting for the music to start.

With his eyes closed, he let out a gentle sigh as the music started to play. When Marvin Gaye asked 'What's Going On,' his eyes shot open wider than an owl's.

"What the fuck?" he yelled, snatching the earphones out of his ears. Looking at the iPod in disbelief, he checked again for the chipped corner.

"Fuck!" he yelled out again, sitting up on the bed.

The Haters. They did it. They took the damn thing and changed my music. Fuck that. I'll get their asses, he was thinking as he got out of the bed only to see the clock on the dresser telling him it was 10:00 p.m., which would make him one hour late to pick up Kim.

"Shit, Kim," he continued, making a split decision to go get her and deal with the Haters later.

CHAPTER SEVEN

Walking faster than he normally would have, he opened the door and practically ran to the stairs, not bothering to hold onto the banister. Taking the stairs two at time, reaching the bottom faster than he ever did, he continued to run to the closet where his coat and boots were. Putting them on quickly, only taking time to check for his keys and wallet, Steven stuffed the iPod in his coat pocket before sprinting out the door without saying good night to anyone or even noticing how quiet and dark the house was before he went out.

Once outside, he went around the corner to where he parked his car, only to find it was not there. Winston, who had the extra set of keys, must have taken it, he reasoned. He decided to go down to the main intersection to get a taxi instead of trying to borrow one of his brothers' cars. This way, if he had too much to drink, he would not have to drive home.

With the way he was feeling, he planned to drink a lot.

At the intersection, there was always a taxi to be had, which is why he did not have to wait five minutes before one pulled up to him. When he jumped into the back seat, he was not surprised to see a passenger already in the front seat. The drivers did this a lot to make more money.

"Wat up?"

"You got it, my brother," the driver responded.

The passenger just looked back and nodded.

"Yo, man, I'm in a rush. I'll pay you extra if you could drop me off first, of course, if he doesn't mind?"

"Ah, man, it's cool. He's with me. Where you going?"

"To Vermont Avenue, over on the East Side. You know where that's at?"

"Yeah, man, I know where it is, but it's going to cost you ten bucks."

Ten dollars? Steven thought, thinking he would be paying at least twenty-five.

"Yeah, that's cool. I got it, but check it out. I'm going to get my girl and then back over to Elmont Street. Can you do that?"

"Yeah, man, for five extra we got you. I'll take the expressway to save some time."

"Cool," he said and sat back in the seat, going through his big coat, looking for his cell phone to call Kim.

Reaching under the seat, the driver pulled out his gun, and placed it between his legs. He had been watching Steven and wondered why he had on such a big coat on a not-so-very-cold evening. Searching for his cell, he thought he might be searching for a gun.

"What's the matter, Youngblood?" the driver asked, releasing the safety on the gun.

"Nothing. Just looking for my cell phone."

Youngblood? Damn, this guy must be strictly old school, he thought.

"Man, you can afford one of those things?" the passenger asked with a surprised look on his face.

"Yeah, man. Everybody has one. Don't you?"

"Nah, man. I can't afford that shit."

"Shit, I can't either," the driver said, wheeling the car onto the highway and then putting his gun back under the seat.

Steven tried to relax, feeling the car pick up speed. He watched as the passenger lit what he thought to be a cigarette until he smelled the aroma of pot. He took a hit or two, and then passed the joint to Steven.

"You want a hit, man?"

He did smoke and did want some, but was not used to it being rolled in paper. He and his crew always used blunts.

What the hell, he figured, taking the joint from him. After a couple of hits, he started to cough. It was stronger than he was used to.

The driver and his friend could not stop laughing at him.

"Damn, this some good shit," he said in between coughs, passing it to the driver, who had turned to get it from him, taking his eyes off the road for a split second. When he had it between his fingers, they all heard the loud boom of the tire blowing out. The car started spinning and skidding out of control, banging against the guardrail, coming to rest fifty yards from the Beach Street exit.

Steven sat there stunned, not knowing exactly what had happened. The driver immediately put the car in park, turned the engine off, opened the door, and got out of the car, followed by his friend. The car was pinned against the guardrail, forcing him to use the driver's side also. Steven was still in the back seat, finding it hard to gather his thoughts from the combination of the crash and the strong pot. It was then that he realized the laughter he heard was not coming from his head, but from the driver and the passenger. They were walking quickly away from the car, still smoking the joint. He opened the door, climbed out of the car, and followed after them. When he caught up to them at the top of the exit ramp, they were still laughing.

"What the fuck is wrong with you niggas? We could have been killed and you two are up here laughing!"

Running up on him, the passenger grabbed Steven by the collar of his oversized coat, pulling him down to his size.

"Youngblood, don't you ever call me or my partner nigger! You hear me, boy?" he yelled at him with an anger in his eyes that Steven had never seen before. He was speaking through clenched teeth, waiting for an answer, when the driver came up behind him, pulling his arm. Seeing the flashing lights of a cop car behind theirs down the highway, the passenger let go of Steven and the two of them walked quickly to the street. Not sure of what was going on, Steven just stood there until the driver called out to him to come with them.

Still he just stood there, not wanting to be with someone who had just put his hands on him, until he turned and saw the cops. He reasoned if it was their car and they did not want to be near it, neither should he.

"If that's your car, why are you leaving it?" he asked when he caught up with them.

"Youngblood, you got a lot to learn. That shit is stolen," the driver told him, walking side by side with the passenger. They both laughed at him again. Walking behind them up Beach Street with no idea of where they were going, he could not help but think how old the area looked—the buildings, the streetlights, even the colors of the street signs.

Maybe the people who live in this area, who were all White, liked the old town feel of things, he thought to himself, not wanting to say anything to his companions about it. But he still needed to get to Kim's house and needed a ride.

After walking three blocks and building up enough courage to speak to them, not wanting to get jumped on again, Steven asked cautiously, "Hey, man, do you know where I can get a taxi?"

They slowed down a bit, letting him catch up. Stepping apart, the driver reached back, put his arm around his neck and pulled him in between the two of them. Steven looked from side to side at their faces, fearing the worst, until he saw their looks of nervousness.

"Look, Youngblood, do you know where we're at? This is the most colored-hating town we could be in. Now look, I got you into this, so don't worry. I'm going to get you out. We just going to stay on this main road so all these people could see us. Ain't none of these White boys dumb enough to do something where people could see. We just got to walk seven more blocks to Howard Street. That's where the Black side of town starts. There we will be all right and you can get a taxi."

With that said, Steven noticed for the first time the people on the street. There were not many, but more than should have been out on such a cold night, which for some reason was not as cold as it was before he came outside. Most had on just sweaters and hats, like the driver and passenger, something he now wished he had on instead of the big overcoat. Not only did he feel warm, he was starting to feel protected by the driver and passenger, as if they would protect him if something did happen. They kept him between them, now walking at a brisk pace.

"So where you from, Youngblood?" the passenger asked, to Steven's surprise.

Looking at them, he realized they were about ten years older than he was. But before he could answer, two vans pulled up to them, one in front and one behind, as they were about to cross a narrow street.

"Kill them niggers!" he thought he heard someone yell as he watched five guys jump out of each van. He stopped dead in his tracks. Frozen. The passenger grabbed him from behind and pushed him in the direction of the narrow street, yelling at him to run. The driver reached into his waistband for a gun that was now in police custody, taken from the stolen taxi. Not finding it there, he and the passenger lunged at the closest guy, pushed him into the others, and then turned to run down the street behind Steven. As he ran, Steven heard the skidding of the van's tires behind him. He turned to see the driver and the passenger running at him, with the White guys, pipes and bats in hand not far behind.

The driver was yelling at him to run, but for some reason, he could not move. He was frozen once again, standing in the middle of the street, watching as the headlights of the van bore down on him. The van was now close enough for him to see the driver's angry face, with his full intent now registering in Steven's mind.

He now realized he was about to die. He could no longer feel or hear anything. So when he picked himself up and saw the passenger on the ground under the wheels of the van in the spot he was just in, he could only do one thing: run.

And run he did. This time not looking back to see the driver trying to fight them off, yelling, "Run, Youngblood, run!"

CHAPTER EIGHT

Running at full speed down the narrow street, Steven's heart was pounding in his chest. He was frightened to death, just as his grandfather was a few hours ago. His mind was racing, trying to figure out which way to go. He did remember what the driver said when they walked up the street—Howard Street, the Black side of town.

He turned right onto the next street, ran parallel to Beach Street, headed for—he hoped—Howard. Before going too far down, he went back to the corner of the narrow street to see if they were looking for him. As he looked up the street, he did see the headlights of a vehicle. Unsure if it was them, he turned and ran as fast as he could in the direction of the Black area.

Not being in the best of shape, he tired very quickly. His legs started to cramp along with his stomach, and he could not believe how much he was sweating. Needing to stop to get some rest and take the oversized coat off, he looked back at the corner just in time to see the two vans turn onto the street.

Jumping over a fence onto someone's front lawn, Steven hid there watching the two vans pass by very slowly.

He tried to remain calm, but his heart was racing out of control. Taking deep breath after deep breath, he finally calmed down enough to think, and to check his coat pockets. First he removed his wallet and keys, then the iPod. He placed all three on the grass in front of him as he struggled to take the coat off in a seated position. Not wanting to stand, for fear of being seen, once the coat was off, he put the keys and wallet in his pants pockets. The iPod he held in his hand while putting the headphones around his neck. "Damn," he said to himself, for two reasons.

The first, he heard a song playing, meaning he left it on and the battery was draining. Second, the song was Billie Holiday's 'God Bless the Child'. He just closed his eyes then turned it off, put it in his pocket, and left the headphones around his neck. Standing up slowly, he looked over the edge of the fence, checking the street in both directions before walking back onto the sidewalk. He turned right once again in search of Howard Street.

Reaching the corner, he checked to see if the vans were still in sight. To his relief, they were gone. Walking at a brisk pace, he stayed straight for seven blocks, hiding whenever he saw the headlights of a car coming his way. After the tenth block, still not reaching Howard Street and still not seeing any sign of Black people, he turned right at the next corner then left at the next and backtracked a couple of blocks.

Steven was lost.

It was now midnight. He finally decided to take a chance on the next car that came his way. He waited at an intersection at a streetlight. Therefore, the cars had to stop at the red light. This way, from his hiding spot, he could see if the driver was Black before approaching the car. He waited twenty minutes before a car with a Black person stopped.

A man drove it and what looked to be his son, was in the passenger seat. They were in a very old black car with four doors. Not wanting to scare them, he walked slowly in front of the car to be sure they could see him before he approached. When he was sure the man saw him, he gestured for him to roll his window down with a pleading look on his face.

"What's the problem, young man? Are you lost?" the older gentleman with short gray hair and a thin mustache asked with deep concern, after he rolled down the window more than halfway.

"Well, yes. I'm trying to get to Howard Street. Do you think you can give me a ride?"

"Howard Street? The only Howard Street I know is over in the next county, and that is a two-hour drive from here."

Steven looked at him, shocked, not knowing what to say, but hoping the old man was wrong. "Look, you don't want to be out here in these parts at any time of day," the man continued. "Why don't you get in and we'll try to figure this thing out."

Steven did the only thing he could do: he opened the back door and got in the car.

"I'm Earl, Earl Thomas from Chicago, and this is my uncle, Mister Henry Reed. Everybody calls him Mister, isn't that right, Uncle Henry?" the boy said after he turned around in his seat, putting his hand out to shake Steven's.

"Yes, that is right, Earl," he answered without taking his eyes off the road. "So young man, now that you know who we are, who might you be?"

"I'm Steven, Steven Green from the West Side."

"What you doing out here so late, Mr. Green, walking by yourself and all?" Mister asked, still without taking his eyes off the road. "You not in some sort of trouble, are you?"

"No, sir, I'm just trying to get to my girlfriend's house, but the car I was in broke down. I started walking and I guess I got lost," he told him without mentioning the driver and passenger who had saved his life.

"Yes, indeed you are lost. I'll tell you what, since it's so late, why don't you stay the night with us, and in the morning I have to go over to the West Side to drop Earl here to the train station. Be no problem for me to drop you off, too."

"That's nice of you, but I really need to get to my girl's house. Do you know where I could get a taxi?"

"This time of night? Around here? No, I don't think so. You don't know where you are, do you?"

Well, at least I'm safe, Steven thought. *When I tell her what happened, she'll understand.*

"Okay, Mister Reed, you're right. I'll stay over your house tonight. Thank you very much for all your help."

"You're welcome, young man, and Mister will be just fine."

They drove in the dark of night for another twenty minutes or so. Steven trusted these strangers rather than staying on the streets of the nigger-hating town. They pulled in front of a small farmhouse that Steven really could not see in the dark. The only landmark was the big oak tree in the front yard.

"This is it, young man," Mister said to him when he stopped the car. "This house has been in my family for more than one hundred years. I was born in it. It's not much, but it's home."

Earl was the first one in the house. With his back to Steven, he yelled out to him, "Come on, I'll show you where to sleep and get you set up for the night."

Steven was right behind him, tired from all the walking and running. He just wanted to get cleaned up and get some sleep. Walking in the house before Mister, he noticed immediately it was made completely of wood. There was a living room space to the right with very little furnishings, a small kitchen to the left with what looked like a wood-burning stove and a small room in the back with a big tub in the middle of floor. When he was told the bathroom was out back, he just shook his head and thanked God he only had to be there one night.

Mister lit the stove to heat up the house and brought in some water from the well out back so they could get cleaned up. He just assumed they were very poor people, so he did not ask for a phone or why there was no TV. Steven was grateful for their help. However, he would not tell them that they may have saved his life.

Earl took him upstairs to show him the room they would share for the night. There was only one bed, but it was big enough for the two of them, one small dresser, one closet, and one window overlooking the back of the house. Earl sat on the bed, telling him about Chicago as Steven stood at the window.

Looking off into the distance, he thought about how much he missed Kim and how he would do all the things he wanted with his life when he got back home. After his near-death experience, he was more determined than ever. Earl, realizing Steven was paying him no attention, excused himself and went downstairs with Mister. Steven, happy to see him go, took off his boots and sweater, then put his wallet, along with his keys and the iPod, on the dresser. He laid across the neatly made bed, placed his head on the lumpy pillow, and tried to relax for the first time since the iPod went missing.

He laid there, and within twenty minutes, fell into a sound sleep. The only problem was the bad dream he was having. He was hearing loud voices coming from White men yelling, "This little nigger needs to learn a lesson," he thought he heard them say.

Along with the voices of other people screaming, "No, he didn't mean any harm. Please just beat him. Don't kill him, please." However, when he heard Earl begging someone not to take him, he knew he was not dreaming. He jumped out of the bed and ran down the stairs to see two White men dragging Earl out of the door by his neck and Mister on the floor bleeding from the head.

He ran to the door, only to see them speeding off with Earl kicking and screaming in the trunk of their car. He came back into the house, yelling for Mister to give him the keys to the old car.

"They're on the table," Mister was barely able to tell him, still in pain from the blow to the head.

Steven raced out, yelling to him to call the cops, as he jumped behind the wheel and started the car with one turn of the key.

Pulling out to the road, he looked both ways just in time to catch a glimpse of the taillights of the car carrying Earl Thomas to his inevitable fate. He turned right, following the car deeper into the countryside. He did not know who the men were, and for that matter, he did not know Earl or Mister. He only knew the men's intentions, and was determined to stop them.

Following the car from a safe distance for about three miles, he watched them pull off the road, stopping the car in front of a large white barn. He turned off the headlights and drove the car as close as he dared, not wanting to be seen. When he was close enough, he stopped the car and got out. Quickly and quietly he walked in a crouched position to the barn in his stocking feet. Steven left the house so fast he did not stop to put his boots back on.

When he got to the barn doors, he could hear Earl's screams coming from inside. He tried to push open the doors, but found them locked. He went around the left side, looking for a window, but there was none. Running to the back, he found what appeared to be an opening on the second level, but there was no way for him to get to it. All he could do was climb a nearby tree and hope to get a look inside. Halfway up, he balanced himself on a branch right in front of the opening. From there, he was able to see Earl.

Steven's mouth fell open in disbelief at what his eyes were seeing. The two White men stood over him, both with large bats in their hands that were stained with Earl's blood. One of them had a gun in the waist of his pants. They had him tied to a chair, his hands in the back, and his shirt ripped off. Steven could see his small chest going up and down as he gasped for air. He sat in the tree in shock at the sight of Earl's left eye socket smashed in, with blood dripping from the back of his swollen head. Blood now covered his face and most of his body.

"How you like that, nigger? How you feel now, nigger? Come on nigger, talk now, talk now, nigger," the bigger of the two asked Earl, as the two of them stood over him admiring their handiwork. When Earl did not answer, one of them raised his bat, smashing Earl in his ribs, surely breaking them. The other let out a loud howl of joy at this sight.

Steven sat with tears in his eyes as he could only watch as two grown men beat a boy of no more than fourteen to death. The howler walked over to his partner and, without a word, took the gun from his waist then walked back to Earl, pushing him onto his back. They both looked down on him as the howler pointed the barrel of the gun at what was left of Earl's face.

"No!" Steven yelled at the top of his lungs, realizing what was about to happen. The two men turned, and ran to the opening to see him sitting in the tree.

The howler raised the gun at him, shooting at the branch one moment after he jumped to the ground. They ran, almost knocking each other down the stairs and out the barn door to see the old black car pulling into the street.

"I know whose car that is," the bigger of the two said. "Don't worry. We'll get him, too!"

When they got back to Earl, they found him motionless, his mouth open, and full of his own blood.

The howler went to him, kicking him in the stomach.

"Damn nigger died before I could kill him," he told his partner when he realized Earl was dead.

He then stepped closer to his body and emptied the remaining bullets into his face. They untied his body from the chair then dragged it to the stairs and let it roll down to the floor. They then dragged it to the car and put it in the trunk. The two drove Earl's lifeless body down to the river, weighed it down with large rocks, and threw him into his watery grave.

Steven watched the whole process from his hiding spot in the bushes.

He went back to the car armed with enough information, he thought, to get them arrested and sent to jail. Steven was willing to stay in this racist town to testify at their trial if that is what it took to avenge Earl's death.

He drove down the dark road, heading back to the house to get Mister so they could go to the police to start the process of justice. Along the way, he spotted a police car in the parking lot of an all-night diner. He pulled in looking for an officer. After he parked, he jumped out of the car, and ran inside. He found four people, two guys having coffee at one of the three tables and an officer talking to the counter girl.

"Officer! Officer!" he yelled, all eyes turning to him.

"Hey, slow down there, fella," the officer standing said, putting his left arm up in a stop-sign fashion and letting his right hand slide to his holstered gun. The counter girl, who had been leaning on the counter, flirting with the officer, stood up and eased back as the coffee guys got out of their seats slowly.

"They killed him. They killed him. You have to help me," Steven kept yelling, getting closer to the officer. He was not sensing their fear until the officer stepped into his path, placing the palm of his left hand in his chest stopping him from getting closer.

The gun was now pointed at his face.

"Now, who killed who?" the officer asked when Steven realized what was going on and stopped approaching him.

Taking one step back and putting his hands down, he told them the whole story, beginning with them grabbing Earl from the house to them dumping his body in the river. After he was finished, the counter girl—who seemed to be amused by it—stood there with a grin on her face as the police officer, looking concerned, walked over to him.

"I can't believe it. In this town? Well, we don't go for that shit here. What about Mister? Is he okay? I've known him my whole life. Tell me, did you or him call the police?"

"I told him to call when I went to follow them. I don't know if he did or not."

"That's okay, because you told me and I'm not going to let them get away with it. Now this is what I want you to do. Go back to the house and see if he's okay. My partner is in the bathroom. When he comes out, we'll come to the house to get more information from you two."

"Okay," Steven said as the officer put his arm around his shoulder and guided him to the door.

"Hey, boy, where are your shoes?"

"No time to put them on."

The officer stepped back into the diner and closed the door. He walked to the counter and pointed to his cup for a refill from the counter girl as the coffee guys looked at him with grins on their faces.

CHAPTER NINE

When he reached the house, Steven ran inside to find Mister sitting on the couch, holding his head.

"Did you call the cops?"

"No. I don't have a phone. I was waiting for you to get back so we could drive down to the station."

"Don't worry. I saw a policeman in the diner. He and his partner are on their way down here now. He said he knows you and he's not going to let those men get away with what they did to Earl."

"Where is he? Did you find him? What did they do to him?"

Steven stood in the middle of the small room, looking down on Mister, not knowing how to tell this man he met just a couple of hours ago, his nephew had been brutally murdered and dumped into a river. After releasing a deep breath, and with tears in his eyes, Steven said the words Mister knew he was going to say.

"He's dead. They killed him."

Mister bowed his head at the words, letting the tears roll down his cheeks.

"He was a good boy. He was. They didn't understand him. He didn't mean anyone harm."

He said these words as if talking aloud to himself. Steven went to him, bending down, taking his head in his hands and placing it on his shoulder.

They cried in each other's arms for a few minutes before Steven stood up again.

"What did you mean they didn't understand him?" Steven asked, wiping the tears away with the back of his hands.

"Them. The damn racists in this town. Where he comes from, people talk different than the people here. It's really my fault. I should not have let him go down to that diner by himself," Mister answered, when he was done wiping his tears with a white handkerchief that was in his pants pocket.

"Mister, please tell me what happened down there."

"He liked to talk," Mister answered, after composing himself. "You could see that. Well, down at the diner, he said something to the girl who works the counter. Don't ask me what he said, but she told her boyfriend. He was the smaller one of the two that grabbed Earl, and the other is his brother. They have been trouble in this town all their lives. They didn't like that he said anything to her. I didn't think they would do anything like that. They're crazy. Just plain crazy!"

"Are you telling me because he said something to her, they killed him? What could he have said to make them do what they did?"

"I don't know. Something about how pretty she is, I think. I really don't know."

"Shit, I just came from there. She knows I saw what they did. I got to get out of here," Steven said, backing away, heading for the stairs. "Look, you got to let me take the car. I'll bring it back."

"But where are you going to go? You don't even know where you are at. Go get your stuff and I'll take you somewhere to hide until it's safe."

When Steven reached the top of the stairs, Mister was heading for the door to go get the car ready.

When the door flew open, he could not believe his eyes. The two coffee guys and the killer brothers were being led into the house by the police officer, still in uniform. All of them had their guns drawn.

"Get that nigger," one of them yelled.

The officer aimed his gun at Steven, pulling the trigger just after Mister pushed his arm, causing the bullet to miss him by inches. The officer pulled the gun back, hitting Mister across the head with the butt of it, causing yet another stream of blood to cascade down his forehead. The coffee guys sprinted up the stairs after Steven, and the killer brothers ran back outside to try to catch him in the back of the house. In the room, Steven grabbed the iPod off the dresser, leaving behind the wallet and keys.

He ran for the window, looked out of it, and thought, *here we go again.*

The coffee guys burst into the room just as he started to jump. When they got to the window, they shot at anything moving in the night. Steven was long gone in the darkness, searching for a new hiding place to watch the events unfold, just as he did down by the river.

"Did you get that nigger?" the police officer yelled to the coffee guys and the killer brothers when they returned.

"No. That crazy nigger jumped out of the window," the bald-headed one of the two said.

"We saw him run into the woods. I got a shot off, but I don't think I hit him," reported the younger of the killer brothers.

Holding Mister by the arm, the officer pulled him outside followed by the four of them. In the darkness, he ordered Mister to stand under the big tree. Then he told the brothers to go to the car and get the gasoline.

"I know you're out there, boy, watching, so you listen. We don't want to hurt you. There's been enough of that tonight. So why don't you come out of those woods so we can talk this over? I know we can work this out. I'm sorry about your friend. If I was there, it would not have happened. That's why I can promise you right now. It is over. Come on, boy, let's talk."

Steven could not believe what he was hearing—this coming from a cop who had just shot at him.

Damn, what is wrong with these people? was all he could think of from his hiding spot in the woods.

"Okay, boy, is that the way it's going to be? Maybe you can't see your way over here, so we'll give you some light." With that, he nodded to the brothers, who then walked into the house with the gasoline. When they came out, the canisters that held the gas were empty.

"Tell him to come here now or else," the police officer told Mister, who was standing with his hands tied behind his back.

He raised his head and looked at the house then at the officer, then returned his head to its bowed position, never saying a word.

The four followers of the police officer now held burning branches in their hands. When he nodded at them, they each went to the house. Upon their return, the glow from the fire was so bright Steven was able to see tears running down Mister's cheeks as he stood watching the house that he was born in become engulfed in flames.

Steven stood from his crouched position, his mouth wide open in disbelief of what he was seeing. He wanted to go help Mister the way the driver and the passenger had helped him, but he knew what these five men were capable of doing.

So he stayed there and hoped they would not kill Mister.

"Can you see your way now, boy? Come in out of the woods. It's not too late. We can fix this, but I can't wait all night. You got five minutes, and then Mister is going to need some real help!"

Steven was tormented. While holding his head in his hands, he prayed to God this was a dream he would soon wake up from, and all this madness would never have happened.

"Your time is up, boy. I never could tell time," the officer yelled after only a minute or two. "Go get the damn rope," he directed one of the coffee guys.

When he got back, he tossed one end of the rope around a branch of the tree a couple of times until it was tight. The other coffee guy pulled the car under the tree. The killer brothers got on top of the trunk, pulling Mister up along with them. The older of the two tied the other end of the rope around Mister's neck, making sure it was tight. The two of them jumped off the car and stood next to their leader.

"This is it, boy. This is your very last chance. Now what's it going to be?"

Steven shook uncontrollably with fear as his mind raced out of control with all kinds of thoughts. He did not know what to do to save Mister. He knew it was him they wanted dead.

He watched the whole time as Mister just stood there not trying to fight them and not begging. It was then Steven realized Mister was about to give his life, with no complaints, to help save his.

"That's it, boy. You think I'm bluffing? You think I won't do it? Well, fuck you and this old nigger. Kill his ass," he said in a calm voice to one of the coffee guys behind the wheel of the car. The coffee guy revved the engine once, then put the car in drive and hit the gas.

Mister dropped off the trunk of the car.

His neck snapped back and eyes shot wide open.

Gasping for every bit of air he could get, Mister was not ready to die.

The five of them cheered him on as if it were a game. The police officer then walked to his car, went into the trunk, and pulled out a small metal container. He walked to where Mister was now swinging dead in the night, and tossed gasoline onto his body.

"Boy, you did this!" He took a cigarette and matches out of his shirt pocket, put the cigarette in his mouth, lit it, and then tossed the lit match onto Mister. From the distance, they heard Steven's screams as Mister's body started to burn. They all ran into the woods, shooting in the direction of his voice.

"Oh my god! Oh my god!" was all he was able to get out until he felt the air become hot from the bullets whizzing past his ears. Then and only then was Steven able to come out of the shock of seeing Mister's dead body.

Without hesitation, he took off with no clue of which way to go. He just started running, not caring about his feet, which were still only covered by his socks. He kept running until the sound of the bullets faded away. The last words he heard from the killer five were, 'You're a dead nigger, boy,' spoken by their leader, the police officer.

Finally, after what seemed to be five miles of running and walking in the woods, Steven could no longer take the pain in his legs or his feet, which he was sure, were bleeding at this point. He let his body fall to the ground. Lying there at the base of a tree, he gasped for air. The pain was so excruciating, he almost wished he were dead.

Feeling the iPod pressing against his thigh, he pulled it out of his pocket right before he passed out.

The iPod was playing faintly Biggie's 'More Money, More Problems.'

CHAPTER TEN

"Now who the hell could that be at this time of night?" Winston said aloud to no one in particular when the doorbell rang, bringing silence to the Green family kitchen. He walked to the door, followed by the eyes of the rest of the family. When he reached it, he did not bother to ask who was there or look out the glass window in the door.

Opening it with a stern look on his face, he actually was not surprised to hear Kim saying, "Hello, Mr. Green," as she pushed by him. Taking off her hat and coat, she walked into the house uninvited with a sterner look on her face than his.

What did that boy do now? Shit, lucky the other girl is not here, crossed his mind.

"Hello, Kim," he said closing the door.

She hung up her coat and hat in the closet, then walked into the kitchen, saying hello to everyone in the room.

"Hello," they responded in unison.

"Mrs. Green, is Steven upstairs?" she asked her, not trusting any of the men for a truthful answer, but trusting her woman's intuition Steven was and not alone.

"Yes, I think he is."

Kim had started up the stairs before Ruby had finished saying yes. The Greens shook their heads and smiled at one another as she went upstairs quickly.

"You think she found out he wants to be a gangster rapper?" Russell asked jokingly, bringing laughter to the room.

At the top of the stairs, Kim stomped down the hallway to his room. She passed some of the kids and did not see Pops standing in his doorway. Once at Steven's door, she banged on it three or four times, causing the kids to stare at her. She waited a few moments, and then banged again. This time when there was no answer, she looked in Pops' direction, seeing him for the first time.

"Is he in there?"

"Hello, Kim."

"I'm sorry, Pops. Hello, but do you know if he's in there?"

"I really don't know. I've been in the room and only came out because I heard you on the stairs. I wanted to make sure the kids were okay."

Turning back to the door, she looked down at the doorknob, tempted to open it.

Bang, bang, bang, she pounded on the door then called out his name. After more long moments of being stared at by the kids and Pops, and with no answer forthcoming, she grabbed the doorknob. Expecting the worst, she opened the door and stepped inside the dimly lit room.

Looking around, she could only wonder what had happened. Steven normally kept his room very neat, yet here it was a mess. Clothes were hanging out of the dresser drawers, the closet was open with shoeboxes all over the place, and clothes were all over the floor.

"What's his problem?" she asked herself. She walked to the bed and violently shook his body until he woke up.

Steven started kicking and swinging at her, the earphones falling out of his ears.

"Please, please don't shoot me! Please don't shoot me! Pops! Oh god Pops! I'm sorry! I'm so sorry!" he screamed out.

"What the fuck?" Kim said, stepping back from the bed before he could hit her. "Steven, Steven, wake up. Wake up. You're dreaming. Wake up."

Startled, Steven finally opened his eyes and sat up on his elbows as he tried to focus. When he realized it was Kim standing over him and he was in his room, not in the woods, he closed his eyes again and let his body fall back on the bed.

"Shit, Steven, you almost took my head off. What the hell were you dreaming about?" Kim said after walking to the edge of the bed and looking down on him.

Still laid out with his eyes closed, he took deep breaths trying to calm himself then put his hands over his eyes, trying to hold back his tears.

"Baby, what's wrong? Are you okay?" she asked, sitting on the bed next to him, taking him in her arms.

No longer able to hold the tears back, Steven rolled into the comfort of her body and let the tears fall. She leaned into him, holding him tightly to her chest. Not knowing what had upset him and not caring because whatever it was, she would help him overcome it. She stayed with him for the next ten minutes, letting him cry, falling deeper in love with him than she already was.

"I love you, Steven. Always have, always will," she whispered as she rolled him on his back. Laying on top of him, she kissed him gently on his eyes, tasting his tears. Kissing his cheeks she worked her way down to his neck. He just lay back with his arms over his head. His breathing finally became regular as she continued to gently kiss him on his neck and pulling his shirt out of his pants, exposing his chest at the same time. Sitting up on him, she pulled up the bottom of his shirt, causing him to sit up.

She pulled it up over his head and over his outstretched arms, tossing it on the floor, then pushed his well-built torso back down on the bed. Following his descent, she opened her mouth wide to take his right 'pec' into her mouth, fondled his nipple with her tongue, then sucked on it forcefully, causing him to moan aloud while running his hands through her long brown hair.

"I don't know what made you so upset, but I'm going to make you one hundred times happier. I got you, baby. I got you," she told him reaching back to pull his hands out of her hair, then placing them back above his head.

He closed his eyes feeling her do to the left 'pec' the same she did to the right, tracing his chest with her tongue down to his waist.

After forty-five minutes or so, they laid in each other's arms, she still on top of him, enjoying the afterglow of their intense lovemaking.

Chapter Eleven

Although he enjoyed how Kim made him feel, Steven was still shaken about his dream. When she asked him about it, he lied, saying it was just a nightmare she helped remove from his mind. She hugged and kissed him, telling him she would do anything to make him happy.

"Baby, are we still going to the party? We don't have to if you don't want to. We can go to my place. No one is home. Then I could really show you how I feel about you!"

"Nah, baby, I'm cool. How about we get cleaned up and go for a little while, then we can go to your place and I could show you how I feel about you!"

He did not really want to go at this point, but he knew his boys would never forgive him if he missed this one. There was a chance the DJ would let them get on the 'mic'. Steven had to go. Kim was glad he said yes. She really did want to go. Dancing and drinking with him were like foreplay, which was the reason for the short skirt and low-cut blouse. Kim could not wait to get there.

After they took turns getting cleaned up in the bathroom across the hall from his room, they headed down the hallway. They passed the kids still playing their games under the watchful eye of Pops, who had a knowing look on his face as they approached him in the doorway.

Without saying a word, Steven walked over to him and gave him an extra-long hug, then took Kim by the hand and headed down the stairs very carefully, as he usually did. When they walked into the kitchen to say goodnight to everyone, Steven still had a sad look on his face that Ruby noticed, but didn't say anything about, thinking it was a problem between him and Kim.

"That boy is whipped," Stan said after they left the kitchen, bringing a high five from Winsome, but an elbow to the ribs from his wife who was sitting next to him.

"Steven, it's freezing outside. Don't you think you should put a coat on?" Kim asked at the closet when she was bundled up in her coat and hat. She looked at him as if he were crazy when he started to open the door in only his sweater and hat.

"Oh yeah," he said, looking at what he had on and getting his big coat from the closet.

"Steven, are you sure you're okay?"

"I'm good, baby. Let's go have a good time," he answered when they were in the car, before he leaned over to kiss her deeply on the mouth.

They drove the thirty minutes to the party mostly in silence. Turning onto Elmont Street, where the party was, they noticed all the cars.

"Shit, this place is packed! If someone didn't fall asleep, we would have been early and got a good parking spot. But then again, we would not have made love."

"Don't worry. I will drop you off in front, then go park," Steven responded, still somewhat subdued. The biggest Black fraternity was giving the party at their off-campus house, a huge ten-bedroom old gothic-looking house that sat alone on the dead-end block. There they never had to worry about someone calling the cops because of too much noise. It had three floors and could hold up to two hundred people. Because they were off campus, the school could not police them.

When they pulled up in front, people were hanging out, drinking and smoking. Before Kim got out of the car, they kissed gently on the lips. She told him to park the car quickly because she was not finished with him.

Jumping out, she skipped up to the front door and greeted all of the people in her usual happy-go-lucky manner. Once inside, she got a Rum and Coke from the bar, and then went in search of Calvin, a.k.a. 'C Money', Steven's best friend from childhood. Kim was determined to have a good time, and if anyone could get 'S' out of his funky mood, it was 'C Money'.

Making her way through the elbow-to-elbow crowd, just the way she liked it, to the DJ on the first floor, she found David, a.k.a 'D Love', who told her 'C' was on the second floor holding it down with the other DJ. It took her a good fifteen minutes to get upstairs, mostly because she was too busy talking and flirting with all the cute guys she passed. She called it good, clean, college fun that Steven actually knew about, which he was okay with it because they knew whom she was going home with, and that was him.

Finally on the second floor, she ran into Ronny, a.k.a. 'Ron Bee', the last of their four-man crew. They stopped at the bar and got another drink, and then he took her over to the corner, where 'C' was bumping and grinding to the loud reggae music with a seventeen-year-old gate-crasher. Kim wasn't hatin' on her, but she needed 'C' more than this teenager needed him between her legs. Pulling on his arm, he turned around innocently, thinking it was his girl Pam, seeing that it was Kim, his look changed from despair to joy.

He gave her a big hug and kiss as he always did.

"Where's my nigga 'S'? Ain't no party without my main nigga."

"That's what I'm talking about. Come on, we need to talk," Kim shouted to him over the loud music, pulling him away from the crasher that Ron Bee stepped to, not missing a beat from where 'C' left off.

They went to the third floor where most of the bedrooms were. On their fourth try, they finally found one that was empty. Dragging him inside, she sat him on the bed and stood over him. For a minute, 'C' thought she was going to get at him, something he would never let go down, but the thought went away quickly when she started talking fast and loud.

Kim was upset.

"You better go downstairs and get your nigga and find out what his problem is, because if you don't, no one is going to have a good time tonight. That's you, 'D', and Ron. I'm not playing, 'C'. I mean it. You know how he is when he gets upset!"

"Wait. Wait. Hold up. I don't even know what you're talking about," 'C' pleaded, standing up and looking down at her.

"Well then, I'll tell you." For the next ten minutes, Kim told him every detail of the night's events, even how she sexed him and still couldn't bring him out of it.

"Damn, Kim, what could that nigga been dreaming about? Shit, he sounds fucked up!"

"I don't know, but you better find out and handle it or we could all leave right now!"

Those were the last words he heard her say before she left him standing there.

"Damn it, 'S'," he said out loud, watching Kim walk back down the stairs. She was right. He needed to find out what got Steven so upset and handle the problem. He did not need him pissed off at a party with Kim walking around looking like she did. She was hot, and everybody knew it, except her, he often thought. This was the only reason he figured she was always trying to get attention.

Steven understood this about her, but when he was pissed off, he did not care and they all could wind up getting into a fight. The worst part about it was she never messed with anybody but him. She would just dance and talk with those other cats and always leave with him. Actually, Kim was all talk, but not 'S'. He got down for his.

Steven had to park so far away from the house, he thought about getting a taxi back. The thought left his mind as quickly as it entered. He just zipped up his coat and fought the hawk back to the house. When he got to the walkway, he saw more people there than when he dropped Kim off. They were crowded together with their heads down, catching a smoke.

To get to the door, he had to go through them. Most of them he knew, but had not seen in a while, so it made him feel good to see them. He had his hood on covering his head and part of his face. In the darkened walkway he was unrecognizable.

When he got to the group, he pulled off the hood.

"Wat up, y'all?" he asked, loud enough for all of them to hear.

"Yo my nigga, 'S' wat up baby? Yo nigga, where you been?" most of them said after looking up, seeing him for the first time.

Their response stopped him dead in his tracks, as they reached out to him for a group hug. Steven stepped back, not seeing them for who they were, but for those in his dream—the police officer, the coffee guys, the killer brothers, and most of all, the van mob. With a tense look on his face, he took a defensive stance, staring at them.

They also stepped back, returning the look he gave them.

"Yo, nigga, you ain't got no love for ya homies?" one of them called out, trying to ease the tension.

"Yo, wat up, baby?" he heard 'C' ask before he could answer.

He stepped through the tense crowd, leaving Kim in the doorway to grab 'S' up in a bear hug, then dragged him into the house.

"What the fuck is that nigga's problem?" one of them wanted to know, watching them with an icy stare until Kim closed the door behind them.

Inside the house, the three of them went upstairs, followed by 'D-Love', the teenaged gate-crasher, and Ron, who was carrying a big bottle of Hennessey. They found an empty room and went inside. Once settled, Kim helped Steven out of his coat, sat him down in the only chair in the room, and then crawled into his lap. She hugged him around the neck, not paying any attention to her miniskirt rising up almost to her ass. 'C' and 'D-Love' sat on the bed as Ron laid back against the wall with the teenager rubbing up on him, her arms around his neck and her hip in his crotch. He took a sip from the bottle and then passed it to 'S'.

He just sat there with Kim on his lap, a blank look on his face and sipped from the bottle.

'C' was the first to speak.

"Yo, baby, wat up? Wat you so pissed off about? Somebody fucking with you? You know we can handle that shit!"

"Nah, man. It ain't like that."

"Then what's the problem? You were getting ready to take on ten cats by yourself for no reason. Shit, you crazy, nigga?"

"That's the problem right there."

"What?" 'C' asked.

"I ain't no nigga, that's what!" 'S' yelled back, pushing Kim off of his lap and standing up.

She stepped away from him, watching him walk to the center of the room, with a worried look on her face.

"Y'all don't know what I been through."

"No we don't, so why don't you tell us. Then maybe we can do something about the shit, instead you acting like you want to fight the world."

Steven took a long sip from the bottle, and then handed it to 'C' just as Pam walked through the door with a concerned look on her face, not knowing what all the yelling was about. She walked over to 'C', slipping into his lap the same as Kim had done, listening to Steven tell, in full detail, the dream and the discussion he had with his family.

Twenty minutes later, when he was done, he had tears in his eyes once again. Kim went to him, hugging him tightly, guiding him back to the chair where they sat together as he composed himself, with everyone's eyes on them. 'D-Love', who now had the half-empty bottle, walked over and handed it to him. Ron-Bee, who was half-drunk, went back to playing with the teenager, who was more than happy he did.

'C' moved Pam off his lap and was now standing where 'S' just was.

"So that's what this shit is about? Look, man, it was a dream. A bad one, yes, but still just a dream. You have to understand that was then, this is now. We as young Blacks have taken the word 'nigger' and turned it into a word they feared to death, into a word of respect. Now tell me what other people have been able to do that."

"Look at Puerto Ricans, known as spics, Italians, wops, Irish, some nasty shit I don't even know, but they can't change the shit like we did. Hell no, nobody can. How 'bout the sixties generation and their love, peace and happiness? That was bullshit. Them niggas was about sex and drugs, now most of them are dead or dying from AIDS. And how many of them even went to college, let alone high school? Shit, more of us are in college than they could ever dream of. Mother fucker, you crazy. They *lived* a bad dream and hear you are worrying about having one. Fuck that shit. Look at the music they loved. Marvin Gaye's 'Let's Get It On.' What was he really saying? Let's fuck. That was their shit. Man, they just Haters. They had it hard back in their day."

"Now just because it's not like that for us, they act like we can't think for ourselves. What you gonna do, stop spitting on the 'mic' because they don't like what you have to say? Well then, let me ask you this. Who the hell taught us about free speech and equal rights and to stand up for what you believe in? Come on tell me. Tell me."

"They did," Steven answered, lifting his head to look at him.

"That's right, my nigga. They did. That's right. This is our time to live the way we want to live. Our time to say what we want to say. So you gonna sit there and let them control you like the White man controlled them in their day or, be the man they taught you to be and let them and the White man know we control our own shit and the word 'nigga' is what we define it to be? Shit, man, you know damn well if that dream was real, all you had to do was call us and we would have handled that shit. Nigga, you know we got your back and nobody fucks with my niggas! Shit, everybody in this room is my nigga. Somebody fuck with y'all, they gotta fuck with me. Why? Because all y'all my nigga. Man, you can't let what they went through fuck with you. Fuck them. You know what I'm saying?"

Steven stood up, this time not pushing Kim off his lap and walked over to 'C' with his arms outstretched. 'C' put his arms out and they hugged each other tightly.

"Yeah, man, I know what you're saying. I love you, nigga." Steven whispered in his ear as D-Love and Ron-B joined them. The four of them hugged each other as the women watched with tears in their eyes.

CHAPTER TWELVE

"Yo, my niggas, y'all gonna crack the mic or what?" Pam said before she stepped into the middle of them.

"What? We ain't gonna crack the mic, we niggas gonna tear down this mother fucking house," Steven answered just as they all started yelling 'D-Block-4', their crew's name.

"Yo, yo, yo, yo, my niggas," Kim started yelling to get their attention. When they quieted down, they saw she had the bottle in one hand and paper cups in the other. "Yo, niggas, we gotta toast before y'all do your thing."

"What, you don't think I can handle my shit?" the teenager almost yelled at Kim when she handed everyone a cup but her. Everybody let out big *ahhs* and *woos* at her statement, causing Kim to smile then hand her a cup. After all the cups were filled, they raised them high, with Steven now in the middle of the group.

He made a simple toast that they all repeated.

"To my niggas!"

"Yeah, nigga, let's go do our thing," Ron-B said, then headed for the door.

"Oh no, baby, just one more thing first," the teenager said, pulling him to her then kissing him deeply on the lips. Not to be outdone, Pam and Kim pulled 'C' and 'S' to them and did the same. D-Love could only stand by and watch. When they were done, all three girls kissed D-Love on the cheek, giggling as they did.

Coming down the stairs, Steven looked down at the overflow of people on the floor. At the bottom of the stairs, he saw the group of guys he had encountered outside standing together. He walked into the middle of them, hugging them all. When he was done he headed to join the DJ and his crew. The music was blasting hardcore hip-hop beats. D-Love was the first to spit. 'S' was last. By the time he was finished, all the people from the second floor had crowded onto the first, along with the DJ. All eyes were on him. 'S' had the crowd hanging on his every word and trying to rap along with his free style.

The party had become a small concert that 'S' made himself the star of.

When they were finished, the people were chanting their name and giving them dap and hugs as they walked off the small stage. Pam went to the DJ with her hand out. He handed her, with a smirk, the CD he just made of the performance. She took it and ran to catch up to them as they started back up the stairs with people still chanting their name. The group of cats from outside showed 'S' extra love as he walked by with Kim holding onto him. All together back in the room, they celebrated with more drinks and then decided to go back downstairs to join the party.

The three couples found the darkest corner of the room and were grinding slowly on each other for the next hour or so. D-Love, now very popular in the room, found numerous women that wanted to be with him. Back in the corner against the wall, Steven and Kim were enjoying each other's bodies more than she could ever imagine. Sometime during the night, she had removed her pantyhose and panties. 'S' had her back against the wall with her mini pulled up.

They made love in darkness, surrounded by strangers. With their faces pressed cheek to cheek, he could feel Kim's tears rolling down his face.

"Why are you crying?"

The answer Kim gave him was not one he expected.

"You don't know how good you make me feel, Steven. Not just sexually, but emotionally. I don't think I could live without you. I more than love you, I crave you. I'm addicted to you. Anytime you want, I'll marry you and promise to never leave you. I love you, baby, that's why I am crying."

"Baby, I'm deeply in love with you, too, and I could never live without you. I promise I will never leave you," he told her, kissing away her tears.

He had stopped making love to her, began to fix his clothes and helped her with hers. When they were fully dressed, they went to a quiet room back upstairs. Looking deep into her eyes, he spoke gently to her.

"Kim, after what happened to me today, I realize how short life can be, and I want to spend the rest of my life with you. I want you to have my kids. If you really feel the way you say you do, Kim will you marry me?"

"Yes, yes, yes! Steven, I will be your wife!" Kim answered quickly before grabbing him by the neck and pressing her body into his. They hugged and kissed until they heard the knocking on the door and 'C's voice.

"Hey, if you two are finished, we're going to get something to eat. You coming?"

"Yes, I and my bride-to-be are coming," Steven answered after opening the door.

"Then breakfast is on me, nigga," 'C' told him after hugging both of them.

"Thank you, my nigga, and I'm telling you right now, you're my best man."

They hugged again, then 'C' turned to go back down the stairs.

"Yo, my car is parked down the street," Steven said. "Give us a ride to it, okay?"

"No problem. I'll go get mine and meet you out front."

"Cool."

"This started out as the most horrible day of my life," Steven told Kim after taking her gently in his arms again. "Thanks to you, it's now the best day of my life. I promise to be a good husband to you!"

CHAPTER THIRTEEN

'C' felt as happy as he ever had. The crew rocked the house and had more than fifty orders for the CD of the performance. His main man was getting married, and his girl Pam was by his side all night, showing him much love.

Jumping off the last of the stairs, he bumped into a guy he had never seen before—another gate-crasher—almost knocking him down.

'C' grabbed him so he would not fall.

"Yo, nigga, are you fucking crazy? I should kick your punk ass!" the guy said.

Normally 'C' would have stepped to the guy whether he was right or wrong, but tonight was too good a night for that.

"Yo, my bad, my bad. I'm sorry," he said apologetically.

"Damn right you're sorry, you sorry-ass nigga!"

"Look, man, what can I say? I don't want no beef. You got it, man!"

"Just watch where you're going next time."

"You got it. Peace," 'C' said to him, then walked out the door to find Pam waiting for him on the steps.

"What took you so long?"

He told her the good news, without mentioning what really caused his delay. Pam could not believe Steven and Kim were going to get married. She could not wait to get back to the house to see them. His car was only halfway down the block, but it took fifteen minutes to warm up on this cold night. They sat in the car, kissing and keeping each other warm until the car was ready. When it was, 'C' drove down to the end of the dead-end block and made a U-turn, coming back up to the front of the house. He didn't notice anyone in the parked cars he passed until he saw Ron-B sitting in his car with the teenaged gate-crasher kissing all over him, and D-Love in the back with a chick he didn't know. Nor did he see the three people in the car behind Ron's, a female in the back, and two males in the front.

"That's the punk right there, driving that car," the male gate-crasher who 'C' bumped told his older cousin in the driver's seat when 'C's car passed theirs.

"You let that punk nigga push you around and you didn't do shit," the cousin said. "Boy, I should punch you in the face right now my damn self. What I tell you about these bitch-ass college niggas? They think they better than us 'cause they go to school and shit. You know what I'm saying? And here you are letting them push you around and shit. You ain't nothing but a little bitch!"

"That's right," came from the female voice in the back seat that was a professional boxer. "Shit, I would have kicked his and that bitch's ass!"

"If you don't do something, I'm gonna go take care of him, then come back and take care of you," the cousin threatened, then handed him a 9mm handgun from under his seat before he started the car.

'C' parked the car in front of Ron's. Pam, seeing Steven and Kim coming out of the house, did not wait for the car to come to a full stop before she jumped out and ran up the walkway, yelling out to Kim. Kim ran to her as well. They hugged each other and jumped in a circle as they yelled in enjoyment of Kim's good news.

They didn't notice the cousin driving his car slowly passed Ron's with the lights out.

'C' got out of his car and walked towards Steven. While the girls continued their dance of joy, Ron thought he heard the teenaged gate-crasher whisper, "Oh no," in his ear when the cousin's car passed theirs.

"What's the matter?" he asked, as she stared at the car.

"Hey, nigga!" the male gate-crasher hollered as he leaned out of the window when the car stopped in front of the walkway.

'C' turned around as Steven ran to the girls and Ron jumped out of the car with D-Love.

They all stopped at once, at the sound of the gun blast. 'C' with his arms covering his head, tried to protect himself. He felt a burning sensation in his right upper arm and did not know the car was speeding off into the night. After Steven pushed the girls to the ground, he ran to 'C'.

"'C', 'C', 'C'," he shouted, falling to the ground next to him.

"I'm okay. I'm okay," he got me in the arm. "I'm okay!"

"Don't worry. Don't you worry. I'm gonna get that nigga. I'll take care of this shit!" Steven told 'C', holding his face in his hands. Ron and 'D' were now standing over them. They were greatly relieved that 'C' was okay. However, their relief ended when the night was pierced by Pam's screams.

The four of them turned to see Pam's legs and arms kicking in the air, desperately trying to get from under Kim's lifeless body. The bullet went through 'C's arm and into her back, stopping only after it penetrated her heart, killing her instantly.

CHAPTER FOURTEEN

One year, almost to the day of Kim's funeral—a cold, damp day—Steven was being interviewed by Big Tigger, the host of *In the Basement* on BET. When Pam determined enough time had passed for the crew to start living again, she began to shop the CD of their performance around to some of the local college radio stations. From there, it made its way onto mainstream radio.

After a week of continuous airplay, they blew up, just like Steven said they would. Steven, however, was a changed man. So when he dropped a solo project without one word of profanity or the 'N' word being used, even he was surprised at how well it did. After all the introductions were done, Tigger asked him the question all those in the hip-hop world wanted answered.

"'S', you and your crew come onto the scene out of nowhere with a CD that is not only raw and uncut, but is live. Now that is unheard of, and y'all lay it down like no one before. I mean right out the gate y'all blow up with some of the hardest gangsta rap I ever heard, and you know I done heard it all. Then you drop the solo joint, 'Peace-n-Understanding', which is totally the opposite. The industry didn't want to touch it. The streets said it was soft, but now it's the only joint people want to hear. You're nominated for three Grammy Awards. Your face is all over the place, TV, billboards, everywhere. Now tell me, no, tell the world how this happened. What was your inspiration?"

"Tig, have you ever been afraid? I mean really afraid, afraid you're going to get killed not once, but three times in just one night? Then you realize two of those times were in a dream, a dream so real after a year has passed, you still wonder was it a dream or did it really happen? Then, on the same night of the dream, you come this close to getting hit with a bullet fired from a 9mm by someone Black just like you and me that takes out the love of your life. Have you ever been afraid? Tig, fear will inspire you."

"Now let me save you the trouble of asking me another question the world wants answered," Steven continued. "'S', what happened to all the cussing and the 'N' word in your music? Why you getting soft?"

"Tig, I'm not getting soft. *I got educated.*"

In the dream, I learned for myself what it was like for Black people back in the day to have to deal with extreme racism. To have a White man point a gun at you and call you 'nigger' just before he pulls the trigger. Then to wake up to find yourself looking at a Black man pointing a gun at another Black man and calling him 'nigga' just before he pulls the trigger. And here we are, Black people calling each other 'nigger' or 'nigga' as a term of endearment.

"So, Tig, I went in search of this thing—nigger. I had to find out what could represent a term of endearment and be a calling card for death. I found the dictionary defines 'nigger' as a lowlife person, the lowest form of a human being, and the most derogatory thing you could call a person. So that made me think, why would Black people want to refer to themselves as something the White man considers low? No other race of people considered themselves to be something as low as a nigger, so why do Blacks? Tig, nigger had to be something other than what the White man defines it as. I was sure it was. That's why it was in my music. I did not question it until the dream."

"You have to understand something. No other race of people ever called me nigger in a hateful manner until the dream. And, after the dream, Blacks were still calling me nigger like it was a good thing. Then a Black calls a Black a nigger, and tries to kill him like the White man did in the dream. Tig, I was confused. So I kept searching for nigger. I had to find nigger, for if my Black brothers and sisters say there is good in nigger then I had to find it. So I kept looking in more dictionaries and web sites of all kinds. I had to know, was nigger really a person or an animal, a tree, a mountain, maybe a car, a body of water, something other than the lowest form of a human being? Tig, nigger had to be something good. After a year of searching, you know what I found?"

"No, 'S', what did you find?"

"Nigger doesn't exist."

What 'Steven' found in the dictionary as well as on the internet and so can you:

nig·ger:

Used as a disparaging term for a Black person:

Used as a disparaging term for a member of any dark-skinned people.

Used as a disparaging term for a member of any socially, economically, or politically deprived group of people.

The *noun* has one meaning:

Meaning #1: (ethnic slur) offensive name for a Black person
Synonyms: spade, coon, jigaboo, nigra

Sport: In the first half of the twentieth century, before Major League Baseball was racially integrated, dark-skinned and dark-complexion players were nicknamed *Nig*;

In *Saturday Night Live*, comedians Chevy Chase and Richard Pryor say *nigger* and *honky* to each other in a word-association interview.

When Richard Pryor came back from Africa, he decided to stop using the word in his shows.

Main Entry: nig·ger

Pronunciation: \□ni-gər\

Function: *noun*

Etymology: alteration of earlier *neger*, from Middle French *negre*, from Spanish or Portuguese *negro*, from *negro* black, from Latin *niger*

Date: 1786

1   *usually   offensive:*   a   Black   person
2 *usually offensive:* a member of any dark-skinned race
3 : a member of a socially disadvantaged class of persons

Usage *Nigger;* can be found in the works of such writers of the past as Joseph Conrad, Mark Twain, and Charles Dickens, but it now ranks as perhaps the most offensive and inflammatory racial slur in the English language.

How do you get a nigger out of a tree?
Cut the rope. (From the Internet)

'Steven' found nothing good about nigger.

Let us not forget

Dr. Martin Luther King, Jr.

Assassinated on April 4, 1968, in Memphis, Tennessee by James Earl Ray.

At 33, he was pressing the case of civil rights with President John Kennedy.

At 34, he galvanized the nation with his "I Have a Dream" speech.

At 35, he won the Nobel Peace Prize.

At 39, he was assassinated, but he left a legacy of hope and inspiration that continues today.

Medgar Evers

Assassinated on June 12, 1963.

On June 23, 1964, **Byron De La Beckwith**, a member of the **White Citizens' Council** and **Ku Klux Klan**, was arrested for Evers' murder.

All-White juries twice that year **deadlocked** on De La Beckwith's guilt.

In 1994, 30 years after the two previous trials had failed to reach a **verdict**, De La Beckwith was again brought to trial based on new evidence. De La Beckwith was convicted of murder on February 5, 1994, after having lived as a free man for the three decades following the killing. De La Beckwith appealed unsuccessfully, and died in prison in January 2001.

On November 24, 1954, Evers was appointed Mississippi's first NAACP Field Secretary.

Evers was involved in a boycott campaign against White merchants and was instrumental in eventually desegregating the University of Mississippi when that institution was finally forced to enroll **James Meredith** in 1962.

The admission of Meredith led to a riot on campus that left two people dead. Evers' involvement and investigative work brought about hatred in many White supremacists. In the weeks leading up to his death, Evers found himself even more of a target. His public investigations into the murder of **Emmett Till** and his vocal support of **Clyde Kennard** made him a prominent Black leader.

Emmit Till

While in Mississippi, Till did something that was unacceptable in the rigidly segregated Deep South. He whistled at a White woman -- Carolyn Bryant, the wife of Roy Bryant.

Till's body was found in the Tallahatchie River three days after his disappearance. A gin fan was tied around his neck with barbed wire. His left eye was missing, as were most of his teeth; his nose was crushed, and there was a hole in his right temple.

Nearly 100,000 people looked into his open casket during a four-day public viewing in Chicago. A graphic photo of his face appeared in Jet magazine. The images fueled national outrage and helped galvanize the Civil Rights Movement.

Bryant and Milam were acquitted of murdering Till by an all-White Tallahatchie County jury in 1955. They later confessed to the killing in a magazine article.

Till's murder investigation was reopened in 2004, but a Leflore County grand jury declined to indict 73-year-old Carolyn Bryant Donham. Both Milam and Roy Bryant are dead.

"I have to believe all people involved in these assassinations used the 'N' word."

"Do you?"

The following companies have donated 'Steven' to the following Public Schools in New York City for educational proposes.

1. Port Richmond H.S.
2. Curtis H.S.
3. Susan E. Wagner H.S.
4. South Richmond H.S.

THE Dr. Theodore A. Atlas

FOUNDATION

Teddy Atlas

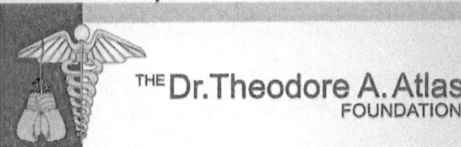

THE Dr. Theodore A. Atlas
FOUNDATION

Teddy Atlas

543 Cary Avenue, Staten Island, NY 10310
Ph: (718) 980-7037 Fax: (718) 876-7037
www.dratlasfoundation.com

543 Cary Avenue, Staten Island, NY 10310

Ph: (718) 980-7037 Fax: (718) 876-7037

www.dratlasfoundation.com

Trucks Roundball Classic

SUMMER BASKETBALL LEAGUE

For Ages 8 to 18

Contact Information

Mark McGhie 917- 385-4276

Truck21hoops@aol.com

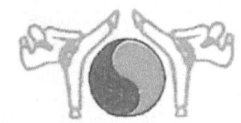

CONROY'S

" EXCLUSIVE TAK KNOWN DO CLUB "

Traditional & Olympic Style Tae Kwon Do

Self- Defense and Ground Fighting

"School of the Fighting Piranhas"

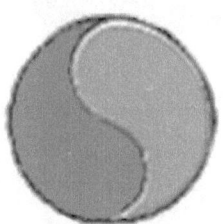

Marketing Administrator

Ms. Kim Weekes
1st Dan Black Belt

1440 Forest Avenue

Staten Island, NY 10302

Phone (718) 442-0034

95

Beautician *Michelle*

BLACK
SWAN
UNISEX
SALON

By Appointment Only - Tuesday, Wednesday & Sunday

Thrus. & Fri. 5:30 P.M - 9:00 P.M * Saturday 6:30 a.m -6:30 P. M

61 Victory Blvd.
Staten Island N.Y 10301

Cell# 718-938 0190
Shop# 718-815-3171

Relaxers | Cuts | Weaves | Curls and more...

Douglas Franks
Associate Broker

Licensed Real Estate Broker
⌂ Each Office Independently Owned and Operated

585 N. Gannon Ave
Staten Island, New York 10314
Office: (718) 979-3000, Cell: (347) 231-3006
Fax: (718) 980-6046, dfhomes@aol.com
www.remax-metro-ny.com

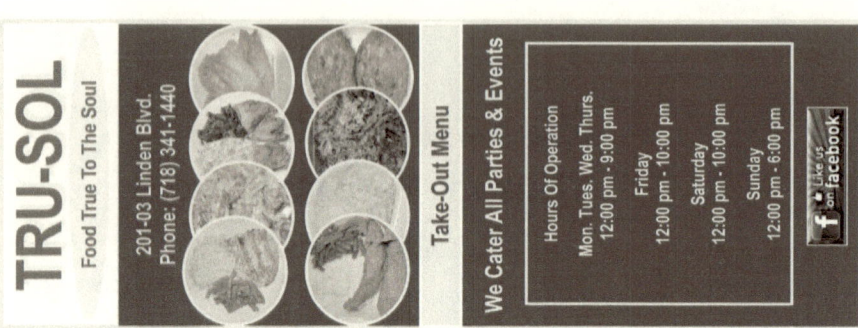

TRU-SOL
Food True To The Soul

201-03 Linden Blvd.
Phone: (718) 341-1440

Take-Out Menu

We Cater All Parties & Events

Hours Of Operation

Mon. Tues. Wed. Thurs.
12:00 pm - 9:00 pm

Friday
12:00 pm - 10:00 pm

Saturday
12:00 pm - 10:00 pm

Sunday
12:00 pm - 6:00 pm

Like us on facebook

Lunch Specials
Mon – Fri 12:00pm - 5:00pm

2 Hot Dogs & French Fries	$3.00
Chicken Sandwich & French Fries	$4.00
Fish Sandwich & French Fries	$4.00
5 Buffalo Wings & French Fries	$4.00
Turkey Burger & French Fries	$5.00
2 Crab Cakes & French Fries	$6.00

TRU-SOL
Food True To The Soul

201-03 Linden Boulevard
St. Albans, NY 11412
Phone: 718-341-1440
Email: trusolsoulfood@gmail.com

Like us on facebook

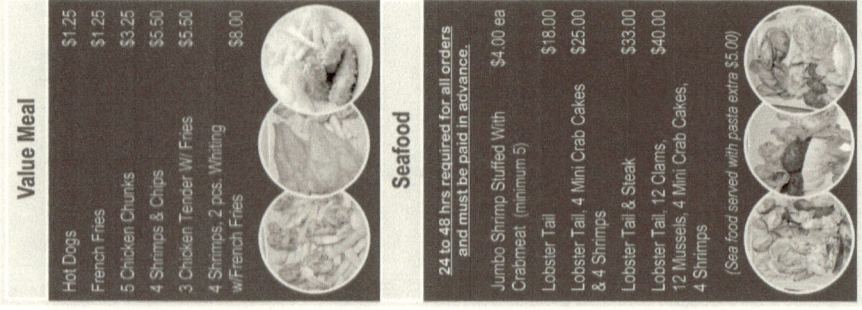

Value Meal

Hot Dogs	$1.25
French Fries	$1.25
5 Chicken Chunks	$3.25
4 Shrimps & Chips	$5.50
3 Chicken Tender W/ Fries	$5.50
4 Shrimps, 2 pcs. Whiting w/French Fries	$8.00

Seafood

24 to 48 hrs required for all orders and must be paid in advance.

Jumbo Shrimp Stuffed With Crabmeat (minimum 5)	$4.00 ea
Lobster Tail	$18.00
Lobster Tail, 4 Mini Crab Cakes & 4 Shrimps	$25.00
Lobster Tail & Steak	$33.00
Lobster Tail, 12 Clams, 12 Mussels, 4 Mini Crab Cakes, 4 Shrimps	$40.00

(Sea food served with pasta extra $5.00)

Sandwiches

Fish Sandwich	$3.25
Chicken Sandwich	$3.25
Hamburger	$3.25
Cheeseburger	$3.50
Turkey burger	$4.00

*****Deluxe*****

Lettuce, Tomatoes, & French Fries (add $1.50)

Individual Items

	SM. $3.00	LG. $5.00
Soup		
Sol Mash Bowl		$5.00
Crab Cakes	(2 pcs)	$6.00
Cat Fish	(2 pcs)	$6.00
Salmon	(1 pc)	$6.00
Tilapia	(2 pcs)	$6.00
Shrimp	(minimum 5)	$5.00
Whiting	(ea)	$1.50
Turkey Wings	(2 pcs)	$5.00
Beef Short Ribs	(4 pcs)	$5.00
BBQ Chicken	(dark meat)	$3.00
BBQ Chicken	(white meat)	$4.00
Baked Chicken	(dark meat)	$3.00
Baked Chicken	(white meat)	$4.00
Fried Chicken	(dark meat)	$3.00
Fried Chicken	(white meat)	$4.00

*Taxes included in prices

Sides

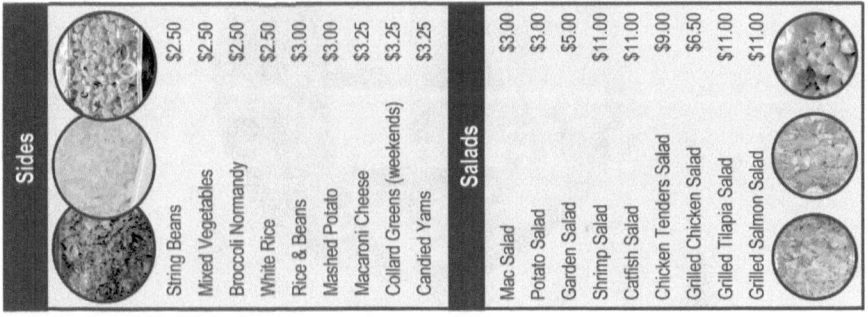

String Beans	$2.50
Mixed Vegetables	$2.50
Broccoli Normandy	$2.50
White Rice	$2.50
Rice & Beans	$3.00
Mashed Potato	$3.00
Macaroni Cheese	$3.25
Collard Greens (weekends)	$3.25
Candied Yams	$3.25

Salads

Mac Salad	$3.00
Potato Salad	$3.00
Garden Salad	$5.00
Shrimp Salad	$11.00
Catfish Salad	$11.00
Chicken Tenders Salad	$9.00
Grilled Chicken Salad	$6.50
Grilled Tilapia Salad	$11.00
Grilled Salmon Salad	$11.00

Dinners

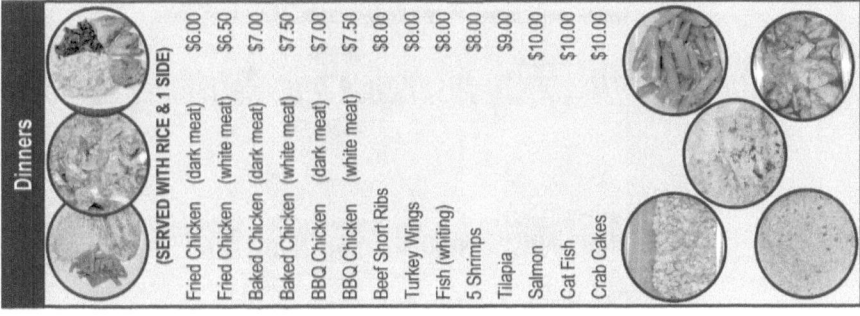

(SERVED WITH RICE & 1 SIDE)

Fried Chicken (dark meat)	$6.00
Fried Chicken (white meat)	$6.50
Baked Chicken (dark meat)	$7.00
Baked Chicken (white meat)	$7.50
BBQ Chicken (dark meat)	$7.00
BBQ Chicken (white meat)	$7.50
Beef Short Ribs	$8.00
Turkey Wings	$8.00
Fish (whiting)	$8.00
5 Shrimps	$9.00
Tilapia	$10.00
Salmon	$10.00
Cat Fish	$10.00
Crab Cakes	$10.00

101

First in Family and Business Protection

Financial Planning for:

Life Insurance, Disability Insurance and Retirement Income

805 Castleton Avenue Staten Island, New York

Tel. 718 - 273 - 9600